16.7
2 ⟌ 33.5
     1
    13

The GREAT Children's Songbook

Edited by David Eddleman
Games and Activities by David Eddleman
Music Arranged by Cindy Fusaro & Dan Fox
Illustrations by Andrew J. Dowty

A Treasure Chest of Music and Activities

(800) 876-9777
10075 SW Beav-Hills Hwy (503) 641-5691
1010 SE Powell (503) 775-0800
12334 SE Division (503) 760-6881

CARL FISCHER®
65 Bleecker Street, New York, NY 10012

ATF121

ISBN 0-8258-3287-X

Acknowledgements

Special thanks go to Miriam Yanes Eddleman, my wife and live-in first grade teacher, who read the manuscript and provided many creative suggestions, corrections, additions, and clarifications. I am fortunate to be the beneficiary of her vast store of knowledge developed over many years of primary level teaching. Thanks and gratitude go also to Richard Kaller, Executive Editor of the music department of Silver Burdett Ginn publishers, for allowing me the use of the research facilities contained in the editorial library there, a library containing one of the most extensive collections of children's and folk materials in the publishing industry and an invaluable resource in researching a book of this sort.

— David Eddleman

About the Songs and Activities

The songs in this book have been selected from many sources by the editors and the author. Often different sources will provide varying versions of the same song. When that has happened the version encountered most often is the version that has found its way into this book.

The one hundred songs in this magnificent and delightfully illustrated collection reflect the diversity of the peoples that make up our musical heritage. In this book you will find songs that represent the spirits of the national and ethnic groups that make up our cultural landscape, including those of African, Spanish and Native American origin. These songs reflect the rich human mosaic of our world.

There are nursery rhyme songs for the very, very young. There are well-known folk songs that have been sung for a century or more by both young and old. There are game songs, lullabies, cowboy songs, songs that teach, songs of greeting and goodby, work songs, spirituals, songs in Spanish and French, rounds for the older children, and patriotic songs. The classified index on page 188 will show you the myriad themes represented by these songs.

There are different activities to go with the majority of songs. Many of the singing, clapping, and circle games have been set down from my own memories as we played them in our schoolyards and in our back yards at party times. A few have been altered to simplify them for younger children. Some activities have been invented and many have been distilled from my own experience in over thirty years of publishing books and music for children. Art activities will stimulate a child's sense of pattern and provide experiences in sequencing, a valuable skill for the young child. Among these activities are two that involve making simple puppets, something that most children adore to do. There are recorder parts to accompany some songs, easy parts calling only for those notes usually taught to beginning recorder players in second or third grade school music classrooms. A singing translation in English is always provided for non-English songs and a pronunciation guide is given as an activity for learning. It is my hope that these songs will be taught by parents and teachers to their English-speaking children to acquaint them with the vast store of cultural variety that we have in our hemisphere. At times, children are urged to use the library to learn more about the subjects of the songs they sing. Many other kinds of activities will serve to enrich the child's day and play.

The accompaniments for these songs, sensitively prepared by Cindy Fusaro and Dan Fox, are simple and easily played by those with a minimum of keyboard skill, and provide guitar chords as well.

May you have as much joy in using this book with your children as the editors and I did in preparing it for them.

David Eddleman

Table of Contents

6

Songs for Any Day

Roll an' Rock

African American Spiritual

Rhythmically

Roll an' rock, — come a - long, — Roll an' rock, — all day long. — Roll an' rock, — come a - long, — My soul wants to go home to glo - ry.

Roll an' Rock

Do a Handjive

You can do a handjive to this song. Just do these motions to each line.

Roll an' rock, — do a hitchhiking motion with your left thumb four times
come along, — do a hitchhiking motion with your right thumb four times
Roll an' rock, — with palm forward, wave your left hand in a circle four times
all day long. — with palm forward, wave your right hand in a circle four times
Roll an' rock, — with your left hand, pat your right shoulder four times
come along, — with your right hand, pat your left shoulder four times
My soul wants to go home to — pat knees four times
glory — clap hands four times

On Top of Old Smokey

American Folk Song

2. A-courtin's a pleasure,
   A-flirtin's a grief,
   A false-hearted lover,
   Is worse than a thief.

3. For a thief, he will rob you,
   And take what you have,
   But a false-hearted lover,
   Sends you to your grave.

4. She'll hug you and kiss you,
   And tell you more lies,
   Than the ties on the railroad,
   Or the stars in the skies.

ATF121

Lazy Mary, Will You Get Up?

Traditional English

Lazy Mary, Will You Get Up?

A Clapping Game

Here is a clapping game you can do with a friend as you sing the song.

First and second lines — On the beat
1. clap your hands together,
2. clap your partner's hands directly (your left hand to your partner's right hand; your right hand to your partner's left hand).

Third and fourth lines — On the beat
1. clap your hands together,
2. clap your right hand to your partner's right hand (cross-clapping),
3. clap your hands together,
4. clap your left hand to your partner's left hand.

Continue the pattern.

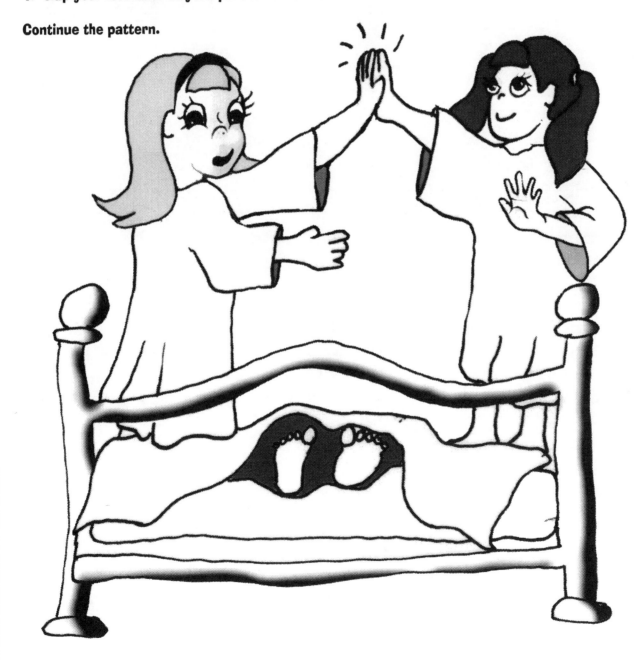

El florón

English Lyric by David Eddleman

Puerto Rican Folk Song

El florón

A Passing Game

In this folk song from Puerto Rico a flower or some other small object is passed from person to person. With some friends, sit in a circle on the ground or on the floor. Everyone sits with hands palm up out to the side. One person holds an object (the "flower") in the left hand. When the song begins the person with the "flower"...

(1) ... takes it in the right hand on the first beat and places it in the left hand of the person to the right on the second beat.

(2) That person does the same thing, taking the "flower" with the right hand on the first beat and placing it in the hand of the next person to the right on the second beat.

(3) The "flower" is passed from person to person until the song ends.

Now here's the trick — everyone in the circle pretends to pass the "flower" from the left hand into the left hand of the person to the right so that no one is sure who has the "flower." When the song ends everyone must guess who is holding the "flower."

If you would like to sing "El florón" in Spanish, here is the way the words are pronounced in Puerto Rico.

El florón pasó por aquí,
Ehl floh-rohn pah-soh-pohr ah-kee,

yo no la vi, yo no la vi (Repeat)
joh noh lah bee, joh noh lah bee (Repeat)

Que pase, que pase,
Keh pah-seh, keh pah-seh,

que pase el florón. (Repeat)
keh pah-seh ehl floh-rohn. (Repeat)

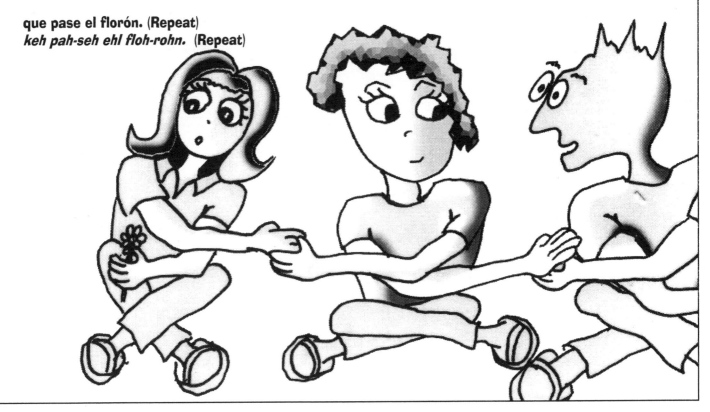

Good Morning, Merry Sunshine

Traditional Children's Song

Moderately

Copyright © 1998 by Carl Fischer, Inc.

Raise a Ruckus

African American Folk Song

Moderately, with rhythm

Come a-long,— oh, chil-dren, come a-long

While the moon is shin-ing bright. Get on board— down

by the riv-er-side, Gon-na raise a ruck-us to-night.

Home, Sweet Home

Words by John Howard Payne

Henry Bishop

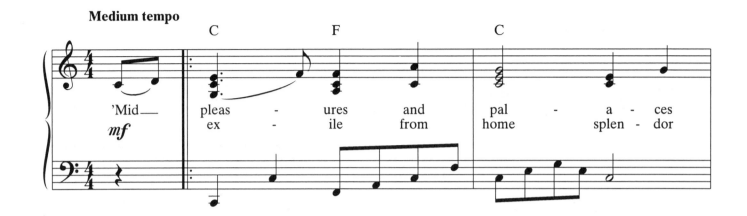

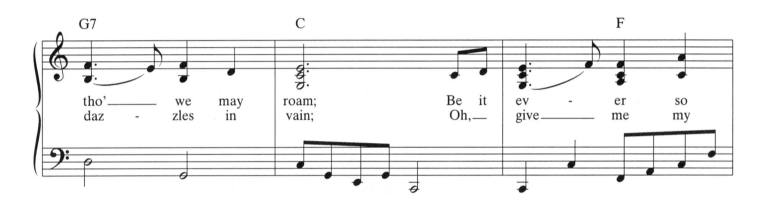

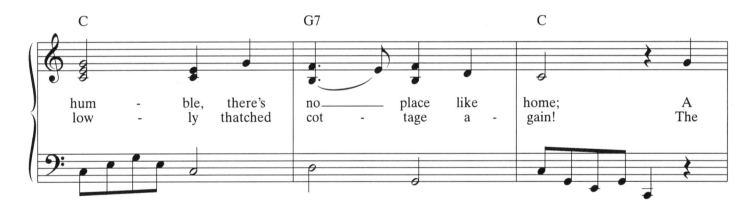

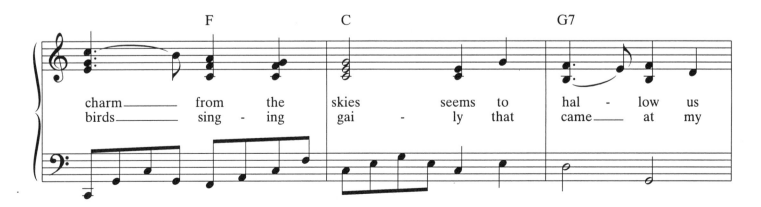

there, which, seek ____ thru' the world, is ne'er
call, give me them with the peace of mind

met ____ with else - where. all. } Home! Home! ____
dear - er than

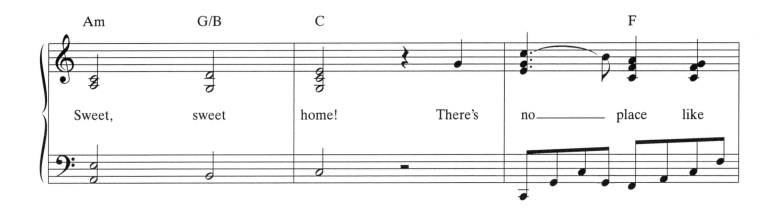

Sweet, sweet home! There's no ____ place like

home! Oh! There is no place like home! An_ home!

Sing, Gaily Sing

Traditional English

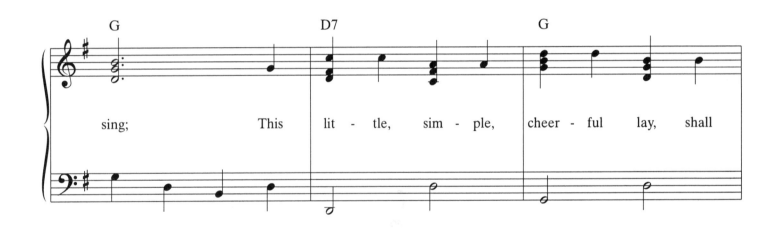

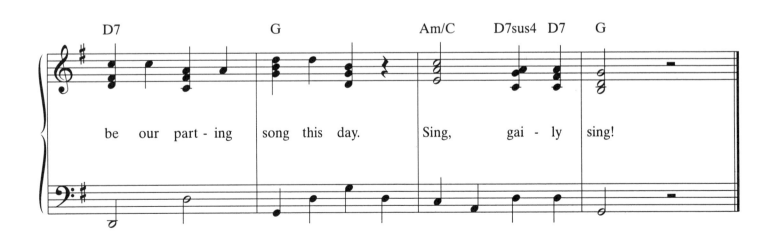

Sing, Gaily Sing

Play the Recorder

Here is a part to play on the recorder while others sing "Sing, Gaily Sing." The part uses only the notes G, A, and B. Do you remember those notes? You probably learned them when you played recorder in your music classes at school. But just in case you've forgotten, here are the fingerings —

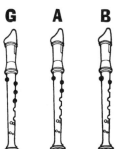

Now practice the part, and then play it while your friends or family sing the song. Don't worry if you make a mistake or two! That's normal when you're learning to play. As you play and practice, you'll get better and better.

Jenny Jones

American Folk Song

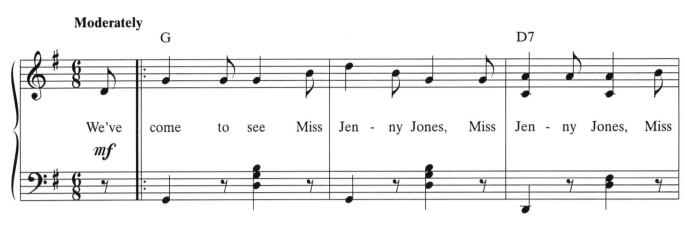

We've come to see Miss Jen - ny Jones, Miss Jen - ny Jones, Miss

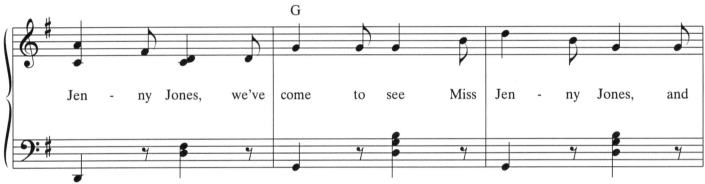

Jen - ny Jones, we've come to see Miss Jen - ny Jones, and

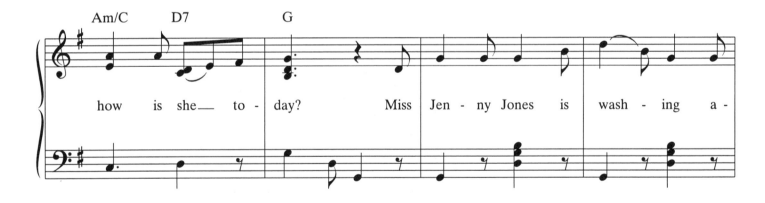

how is she— to - day? Miss Jen - ny Jones is wash - ing a-

wash - ing, a - wash - ing, Miss Jen - ny Jones is wash - ing, you

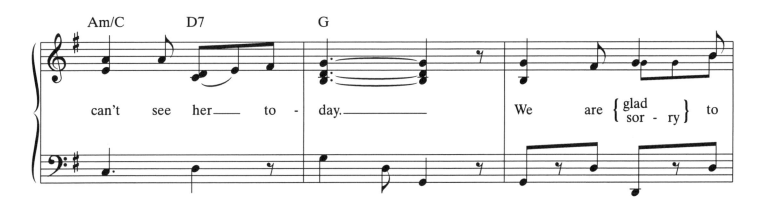

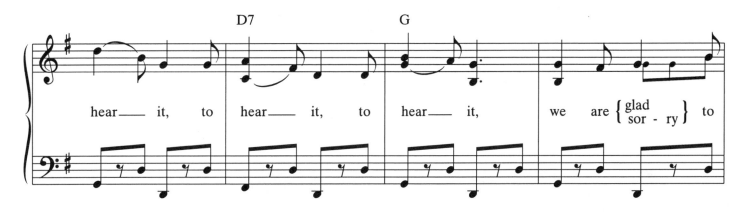

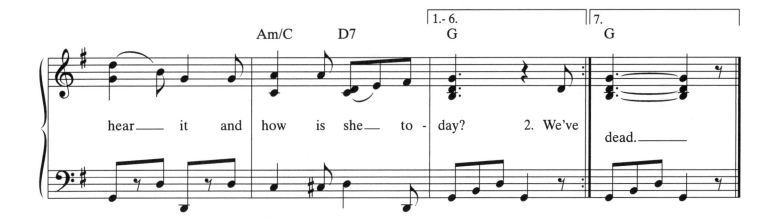

2. We've come to see Miss Jenny Jones...
   Miss Jenny is starching...

3. We've come to see Miss Jenny Jones...
   Miss Jenny is ironing...

4. We've come to see Miss Jenny Jones...
   Miss Jenny is sweeping...

5. We've come to see Miss Jenny Jones...
   Miss Jenny is sick in bed...

6. We've come to see Miss Jenny Jones...
   Miss Jenny is dying...

7. We've come to see Miss Jenny Jones...
   Miss Jenny is dead...

School Days

Words by Gus Edwards   **Music by Will D. Cobb**

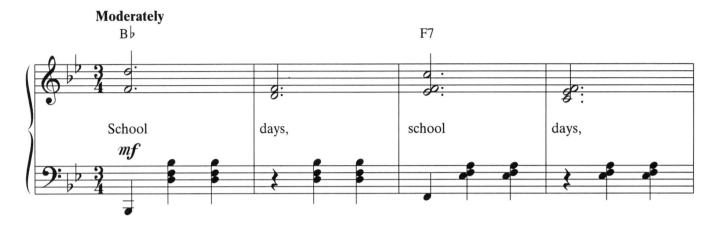

School   days,   school   days,

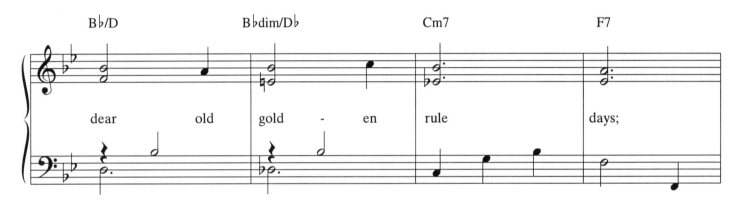

dear   old   gold — en   rule   days;

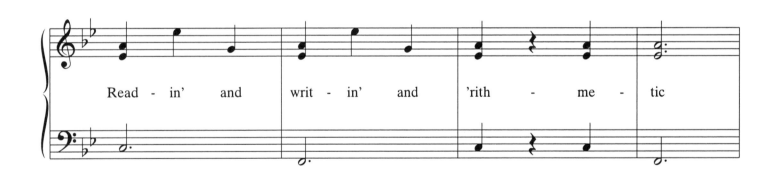

Read - in'   and   writ - in'   and   'rith - me - tic

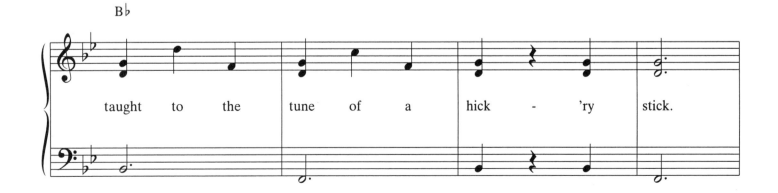

taught   to   the   tune   of   a   hick - 'ry   stick.

Frère Jacques

Folk Song from France

Frère Jacques
(Brother John)

Singing in French

You may have sung this song before in English, but it's actually a song from France and the French words are printed here. It's fun to sing in French. Here is the way the French words are pronounced in France.

Frère Jacques, Frère Jacques,
Frair-uh Zhah-kuh, Frair-uh Zhah-kuh,

Dormez-vous, dormez-vous?
Dawr-may voo, dawr-may voo?

Sonnez les matines, sonnez les matines,
Suh-nay lay ma-tee-nuh, suh-nay lay ma-tee-nuh,

Din, din, don, din, din, don.
Da(n), da(n) daw(n), da(n), da(n), daw(n).

When you see those Ns in parentheses it means they are not really pronounced as Ns. You have to put the sound up in your nose, a little as if you are meowing like a kitten.

Z

Z

Z

Z

Z

Z

z

z

The Mulberry Bush

American Folk Song

3. This is the way..., (3x) early Tuesday morning.

4. This is the way..., (3x) early Wednesday morning.

5. This is the way..., (3x) early Thursday morning.

6. This is the way..., (3x) early Friday morning.

7. This is the way..., (3x) early Saturday morning.

8. This is the way..., (3x) early Sunday morning.

The Mulberry Bush

Moving to the Music

Do what the words tell you to do in this song. Form a circle with a group of friends. On the first verse walk to the left. On the second verse stop and face the center. Pretend to wash clothes as if you were washing them in a sink. On the other verses do the movements that the words tell you to do. Later on try making up some other verses. For example, *This is the way we shine our shoes, . . . comb our hair, . . . brush our teeth, . . .* and so forth.

The Alphabet Song

Traditional

The Alphabet Song

Making an Alphabet Chart

This old "alphabet song" is sung to the tune of "Twinkle, Twinkle, Little Star." On a large sheet of paper write down all the letters of the alphabet in order. You can decorate the letters with crayons or colored pencils. Hang the chart on the wall using masking tape. Then, as you sing, point to each letter as it appears in the song.

For a challenge, write down the letters on small pieces of paper, then put them in order as you sing the song. See what letter you are up to by the time the song is finished.

Did You Ever See a Lassie?
(Song on page 30)

Making Up Movements

You can make up movements to go with the words *go this way and that way*. You can sway your body, turn around in place, swing your arms in front of you or from side to side, turn from side to side, and so forth. You can probably think of lots of other movements to do. Sing the song over and over making up as many movements as you can think of. Work with some friends to think up even more ways to move.

Did You Ever See a Lassie?

(Activity on page 29)

Traditional Scottish

Moderately

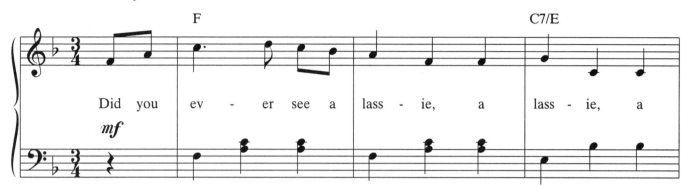

Did you ev - er see a lass - ie, a lass - ie, a

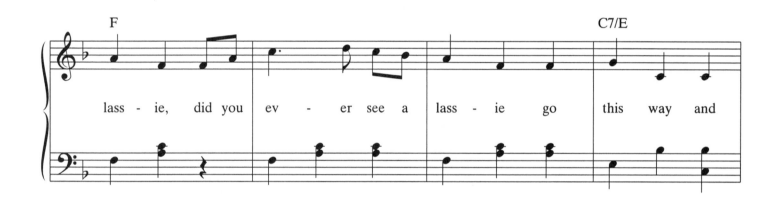

lass - ie, did you ev - er see a lass - ie go this way and

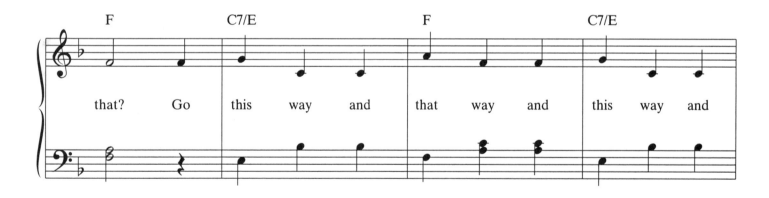

that? Go this way and that way and this way and

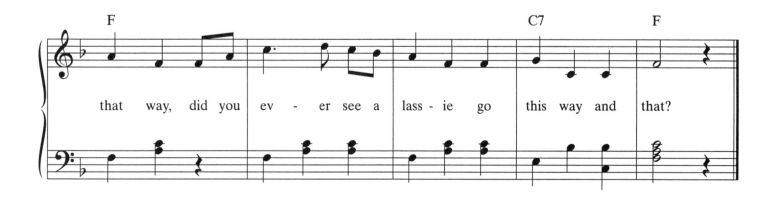

that way, did you ev - er see a lass - ie go this way and that?

Nursery Rhymes

London Bridge

Nursery Rhyme Song

2. Build it up with iron bars, iron bars, iron bars;
   Build it up with iron bars,
   My fair lady.

3. Iron bars will bend and break, bend and break, bend and break;
   Iron bars will bend and break,
   My fair lady.

4. Build it up with gold and silver, gold and silver, gold and silver;
   Build it up with gold and silver,
   My fair lady.

London Bridge

A Singing Game

Here is a game you can play with a group of your friends.

1. Two people stand facing each other with their arms raised and their fingers entwined to form an arch.
2. The other children process under the arch as the song is sung.
3. On the word *lady* the arch comes down and traps one of the couples.
4. That couple becomes the new arch and the first arch couple joins the procession.

See Saw, Margery Daw

Nursery Rhyme Song

Jack and Jill

Nursery Rhyme Song

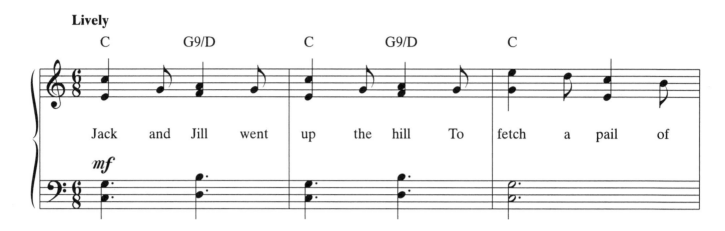

Jack and Jill went up the hill To fetch a pail of

wa - ter, Jack fell down and broke his crown, And

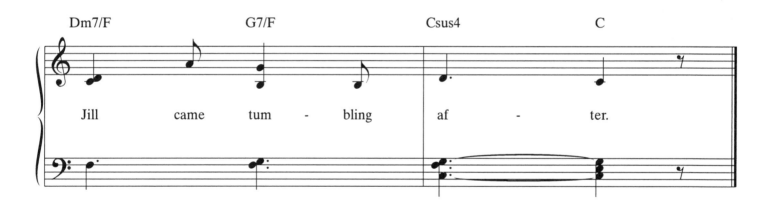

Jill came tum - bling af - ter.

2. Up Jack got, and home did trot,
As fast as he could caper,
Went to bed, to mend his head,
With vinegar and brown paper.

Little Jack Horner

Nursery Rhyme Song

Copyright © 1998 by Carl Fischer, Inc.

Old King Cole

Nursery Rhyme Song

Old King Cole was a mer-ry old soul, yes a mer-ry old soul was he.

Old King Cole

PLAY THE RECORDER

This recorder part can be played with "Old King Cole" as others sing.
It uses not only your old friends G, A, and B, but E as well.
If you don't remember the fingering for E, here it is —

E When you practice this part you will see that it uses half notes ♩ and quarter notes ♪, as well as a whole note ○ at the very end. Remember that half notes are played twice as long as quarter notes, and the whole note is the longest of all. Say the words, *going to the downtown mall.* If you wrote out the rhythm for those words using half notes, quarter notes, and whole notes, it would look like this —

go - ing to the down - town mall.

Now practice the part and try it with your friends or family.

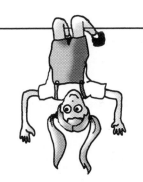

Little Boy Blue

Nursery Rhyme Song

Humpty Dumpty

Nursery Rhyme Song

Mary Had a Little Lamb

Nursery Rhyme Song

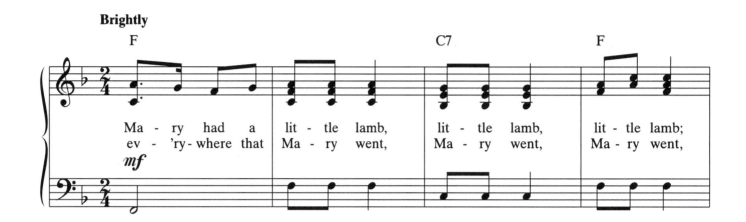

3. He followed her to school one day, school one day, school one day,
   He followed her to school one day, that was against the rule.

4. It made the children laugh and play, laugh and play, laugh and play,
   It made the children laugh and play, to see a lamb at school.

5. And so the teacher turned him out, turned him out, turned him out,
   And so the teacher turned him out, but still he lingered near.

6. He waited patiently about, patiently, patiently,
   He waited patiently about, till Mary did appear.

7. What makes the lamb love Mary so, Mary so, Mary so,
   What makes the lamb love Mary so, the eager children cry.

8. Mary loves the lamb you know, lamb you know, lamb you know,
   O, Mary loves the lamb you know, the teacher did reply.

Mary Had a Little Lamb

Making a Picture Story

You can make a picture with your friends to illustrate this song. You'll need to draw one picture to go with each verse. They might look like this.

A picture of —
1. Mary and her lamb
2. The lamb following Mary
3. The lamb following Mary to school
4. The lamb at school as the children around it laugh
5. The teacher putting the lamb outside the school door
6. The lamb waiting patiently outside the school for Mary to appear
7. Mary petting the lamb as the other children look on in delight
8. The teacher standing over Mary, the lamb, and the children

You can work on this with several friends, each one drawing one picture. When you're finished, present the pictures in order to your parents, teacher, or classmates as you sing the song. It's fun to mix the pictures up and try to place them back in order as you sing the song. Try hanging the pictures in a mixed-up order and pointing to the pictures that go with each line as you or others sing the song. You can also present your pictures as a "TV show" by cutting out a "screen" the size of your pictures from the side of a box, keeping the top of the box open. Then, as you or others sing the song, display your pictures by holding them against the "screen" from inside the box.

Pease Porridge Hot

Nursery Rhyme Song

Pease por-ridge hot, pease por-ridge cold, pease por-ridge in the pot nine days old.

Bobby Shafto

Traditional English

Moderately

Bob - by Shaf - to's gone to sea,
sil - ver bang - les on his knee;
He'll come back and mar - ry me,
pret - ty Bob - by Shaf - to.

Simple Simon

Nursery Rhyme Song

Simple Simon

Making Puppets

"Simple Simon" is a good song to use with puppets. You will need puppet figures of Simple Simon and the pie man in the first verse. For the second verse you will need puppet figures of the pie man holding out his hand for a penny and Simple Simon turning his pockets inside out to show he has none. Simple Simon can be wearing any kind of clothes, but the pie man would probably have on a baker's hat and maybe a white apron. Would he have a pie in his hand? Use your imagination.

After you draw the pictures,
(1) paste them to a sheet of light cardboard, like a shirt cardboard.
(2) When the paste is dry cut out the figures and
(3) glue a tongue depressor or an ice cream stick to the back. You can also use the empty card board tube from a roll of bathroom tissue so you can control the puppet by sticking your fingers inside the roll.
(4) Then, as you sing the song to your parents, your teacher, or to your friends, perform the song as a puppet play using the puppets you have made.

Ring Around the Rosy

Nursery Rhyme Song

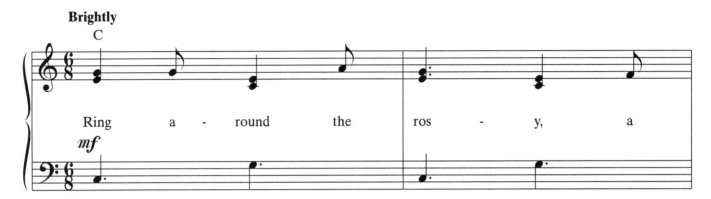

Ring a - round the ros - y, a

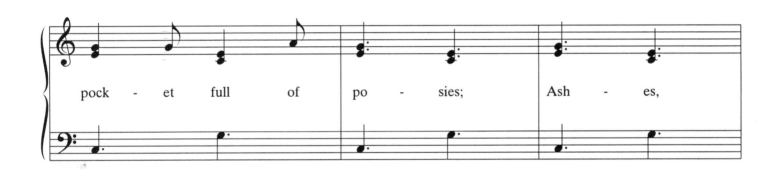

pock - et full of po - sies; Ash - es,

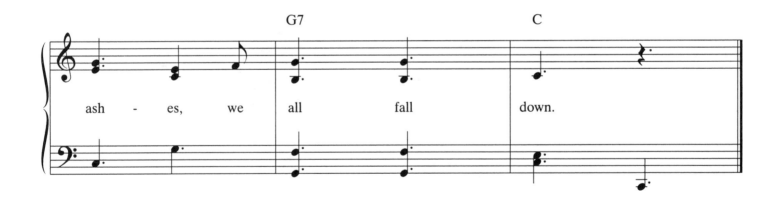

ash - es, we all fall down.

Ring Around the Rosy

An Action Song

You and your friends can do these movements to "Ring Around the Rosy" as you sing.

Ring around the rosy — all join hands in a circle and walk to the right
A pocket full of posies — walk to the left
Ashes, ashes — clap on each syllable of *ashes*
We all fall down — everyone sinks slowly to the ground (be careful you don't hurt yourself)

Baa! Baa! Black Sheep

Nursery Rhyme Song

Little Miss Muffet

Nursery Rhyme Song

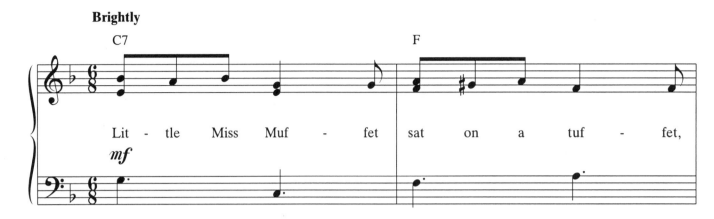

Lit - tle Miss Muf - fet sat on a tuf - fet,

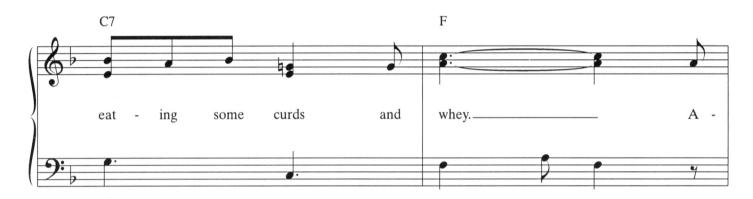

eat - ing some curds and whey._____ A -

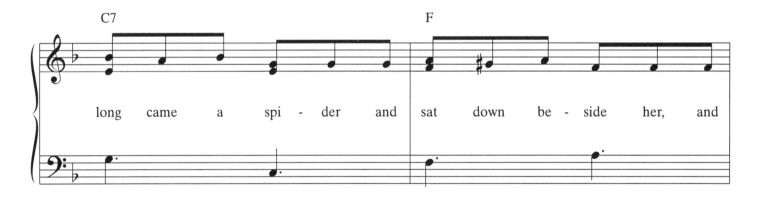

long came a spi - der and sat down be - side her, and

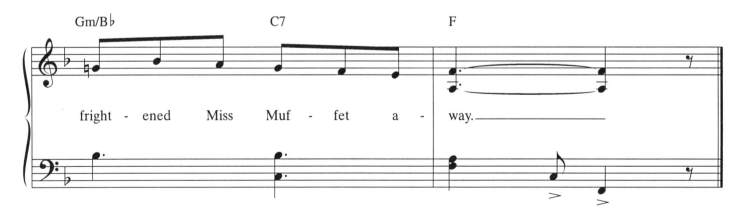

fright - ened Miss Muf - fet a - way._____

Sing a Song of Sixpence

Nursery Rhyme Song

Copyright © 1998 by Carl Fischer, Inc.

Mistress Mary, Quite Contrary

Nursery Rhyme Song

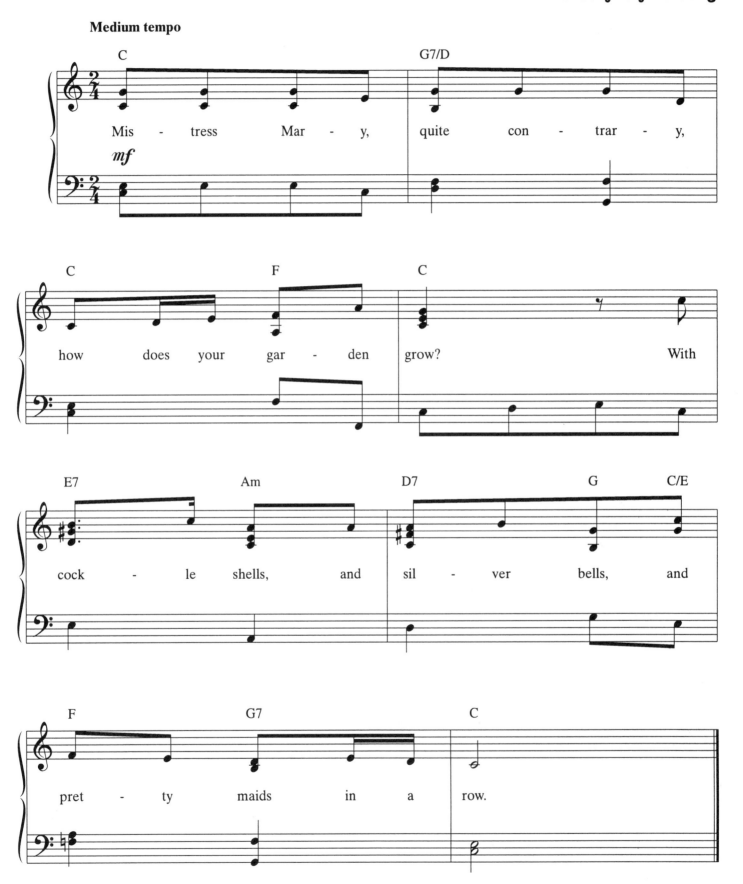

Hot Cross Buns

Nursery Rhyme Song

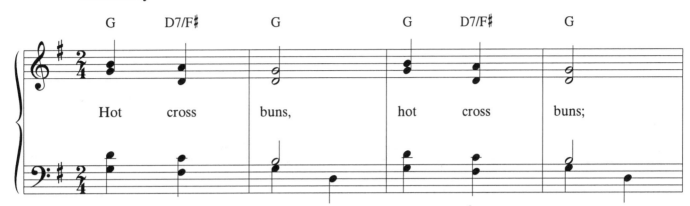

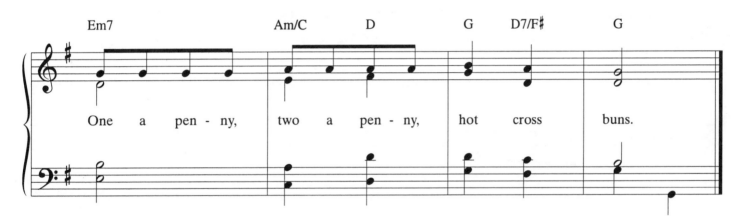

Hot Cross Buns

Play the Recorder

You can play all the melody of "Hot Cross Buns" using just G, A, and B. Sing the melody first and then try playing it on your recorder. The melody uses three kinds of notes —
half notes ♩, quarter notes ♩, and eighth notes ♫. Say the words to yourself in rhythm and you will see how the notes match the rhythm of the song.

ATF121

Pat-A-Cake

Nursery Rhyme Song

Little Bo-Peep

Nursery Rhyme Song

Hickory Dickory Dock

Nursery Rhyme Song

Hickory Dickory Dock

Make a Picture Story

Make a set of drawings to go with "Hickory Dickory Dock." You will need to make five drawings.

Drawing 1 — a picture of a Grandfather clock
Drawing 2 — a picture of a mouse running up the clock
Drawing 3 — a picture of the clock striking one (with a surprised mouse)
Drawing 4 — a picture of the mouse running down the clock
Drawing 5 — a picture of a Grandfather's clock, the mouse sitting at its foot

Sing the song for your parents, your teacher, or your friends, and show each picture to illustrate what happens in the song. Try mixing the pictures up and putting them back in the right order. Hang them up out of order and then point to the right picture as you or others sing the song.

You can dramatize "Hickory Dickory Dock" for your parents, teacher, or friends. Make a big picture of a Grandfather clock on chart paper. You can tape two pieces of chart paper together if you wish to make a really big clock picture. Then you be the mouse. On the first line, *Hickory dickory dock*, make "whisker" movements on your face with your fingers. On *The mouse ran up the clock* pretend to run up to the top of the clock. At the words *The clock struck one*, jump up and clap your hands once above your head, and at *and down he run* pretend to run down the other side of the clock. On the last *Hickory dickory dock*, make your "whisker" movements again.

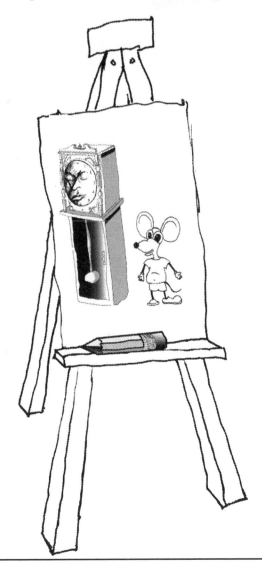

Little Sally Water

Lit-tle Sal-ly Wa-ter, sit-ting by the sun, Cry-ing and weep-ing— for a nice young man. Rise, Sal-ly, rise, wipe off your eyes; Fly to the East, fly to the West; Fly to the one— you— love the best.

Weather and Seasons

Calendar Song

Traditional

2. Fifty-two weeks make a year, soon a new one will be here;
Twelve long months a year will make, say them now without mistake:
Thirty days hath each September, April, June and cold November;
All the rest have thirty-one; February stands alone.

3. Twenty-eight is all its share, with twenty-nine in each leap year;
That you may leap year know, divide by four and that will show,
In each year are seasons four, you will learn them I am sure;
Spring and summer, then the fall; winter, last, but best of all.

Calendar Song

Finding Birthdays

You probably have a calendar in your house to keep important dates recorded. Find out when your parents', your brothers' and sisters', and your grandparents' birthdates are. Look them up on the calendar and write their names in the date box. If the date box is large enough, decorate it with crayons or colored pencils. Is there someone outside your family that you admire, such as a sports figure, a television or movie star, or a musical personality? Go to the library and ask your librarian to help you find their birthdates. You can place those names on your calendar as well and decorate their dateboxes. <u>You</u> have a birthdate, too. Find yours on the calendar and decorate it. You may want to paste a big star sticker on it. Happy birthday!

Las mañanitas

English Lyric by David Eddleman

Traditional Mexican Birthday Song

Las mañanitas

A Birthday Song

This is the song that Mexican children traditionally sing as a birthday song. The words tell the birthday child to wake up and hear the morning bells and greet the sunshine on this special day. You can wish someone a Happy Birthday in Spanish by saying *feliz cumpleaños* (feh-LEES koom-pleh-AH-nyos).

You can sing this song in Spanish. In Mexico the words are pronounced like this.

Estas son las mañanitas,
Ehs-tahs sohn lahs mahn-yah-nee-tahs,

Que cantaba_el Rey David,
Keh kahn-tah-bah ehl Ray Dah-beed,

A las muchachas bonitas
Ah lahs moo-chah-chahs boh-nee-tahs

Se las cantamos aquí.
Seh lahs kahn-tah-mohs ah-kee.

Despierta, mi bien, despierta,
Deh-spyehr-tah, mee byehn, deh-spyehr-tah,

Mira que ya_amaneció;
Mee-rah keh yah_ah-mah-neh-syoh;

Ya los pajarillos cantan,
Yah lohs pah-hah-ree-yohs kahn-tahn,

La luna ya se metió.
Lah loo-nah yah seh meh-tyoh.

Sailing

Traditional English

Sailing, sailing, o-ver the bound-ing main,_____ For
man-y a storm-y wind shall blow, till Jack comes home a-gain!_____
Sailing, sailing, o-ver the bound-ing main,_____ For
man-y a storm-y wind shall blow, till Jack comes home a-gain.

Sailing

A Rhythm Round

Sing this song with a friend. When you have learned it, find a drum (or make one from an empty oatmeal box, using a pencil for a mallet) and play just the rhythm of the words. Then have your friend or a parent sing the song. When the singer begins the second line (*for many a stormy wind shall blow . . .*) you begin playing the rhythm of the words at the beginning of the song. You then "follow the leader" through the song, the singer singing and you playing the word-rhythms always one line behind. You may get lost at first, but you'll have fun doing this once you catch on to it. When you've mastered it you can do this with other songs as well. Experiment to see which ones work best!

De colores
(Activity on page 66)

English Lyric by David Eddleman

Mexican Folk Song

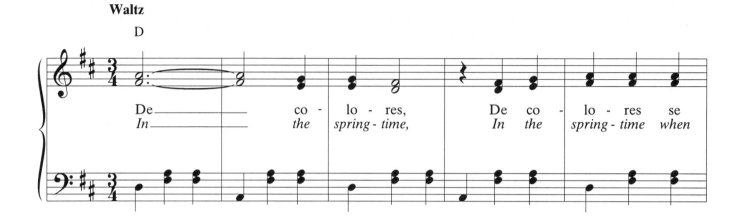

De_____ co - lo - res, De co - lo - res se
In_____ the spring - time, In the spring - time when

vis - ten los cam - pos en la pri - ma - ve - ra;_____
col - or - ful flow - ers are paint - ing the mead - ow;_____

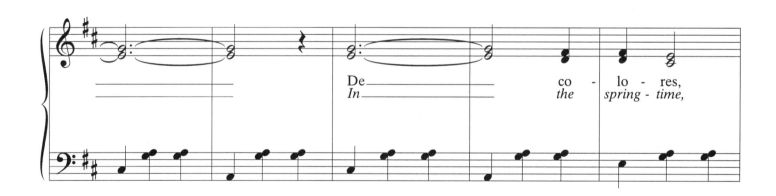

De_____ co - lo - res,
In_____ the spring - time,

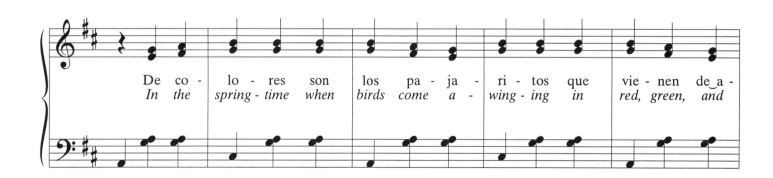

De co - lo - res son los pa - ja - ri - tos que vie - nen de_a -
In the spring - time when birds come a - wing - ing in red, green, and

De colores
(Song on page 64)

Playing in Threes

You can play a steady beat in threes to "De colores." As you sing the song can you feel the beats? They seem to fall into groups of threes—ONE-two-three, ONE-two-three, ONE-two-three, ONE-two-three. Have someone else sing the song while you count the beats aloud. Now find a drum or some other instrument that you can play with a drumstick. As you or others sing, play the beats in threes on your instrument—ONE-two-three, ONE-two-three, ONE-two-three, ONE-two-three.

Want to make it even more fun? Have a friend find another instrument that has a different sound than yours. For example, if you have a drum, have your friend play a cymbal or triangle. Now, as you or others sing the song, you play only the first beat (ONE) and your friend can play only the second and third beats (two-three). You may need to practice to get it right, but don't give up. Feeling the beat in a song is something you'll catch on to very quickly.

If you want to sing this song in Spanish this is the way the words will sound in Mexico and southern California.

De colores,
Deh koh-loh-rehs,

De colores se visten los campos en la primavera;
Deh koh-loh-rehs seh bees-tehn lohs kahm-pohs ehn lah pree-mah-beh-rah;

De colores,
Deh koh-loh-rehs,

De colores son los pajaritos que vienen de_afuera.
Deh koh-loh-rehs sohn lahs pah-hah-ree-tohs keh byeh-nehn deh_ah-fweh-rah.

De colores,
Deh koh-loh-rehs,

De colores es el arco iris que vemos lucir;
Deh koh-loh-rehs ehs ehl ahr-koh ee-rees keh beh-mohs loo-seer;

Y por eso los grandes amores de muchos colores me gustan a mí. (Repeat)
Ee pohr eh-soh lohs grahn-dehs ah-mohr-ehs deh moo-chohs koh-loh-rehs meh goos-tahn ah mee. (Repeat)

ONE-two-three ONE-two-three ONE-two-three ONE-two-three ONE-two-three ONE-two-three ONE-two-three

Eensy Weensy Spider

Traditional Children's Song

Playfully, in 2

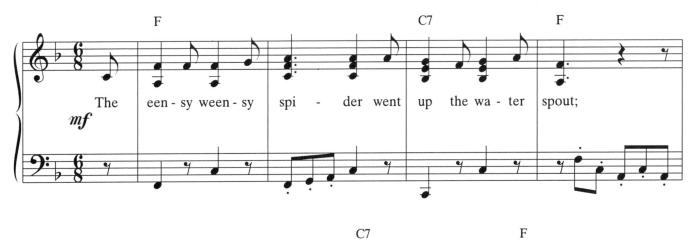

The een-sy ween-sy spi - der went up the wa-ter spout;

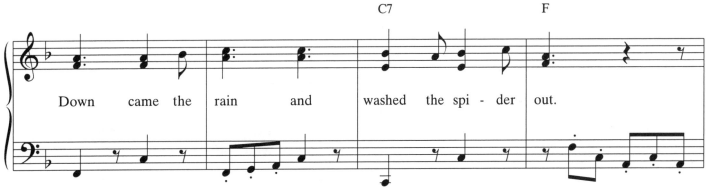

Down came the rain and washed the spi - der out.

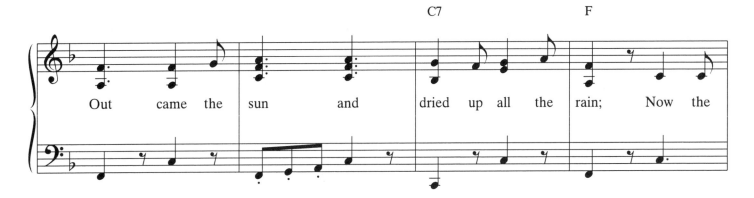

Out came the sun and dried up all the rain; Now the

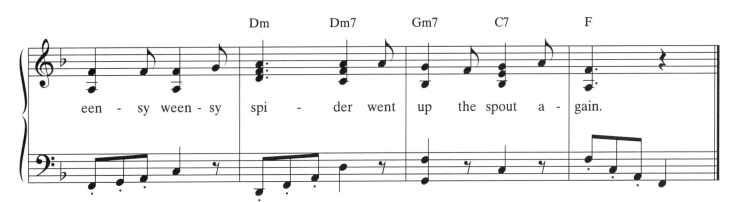

een - sy ween-sy spi - der went up the spout a - gain.

ATF121

El capotín

(Activity on page 70)

English Lyric by David Eddleman

Puerto Rican Folk Song

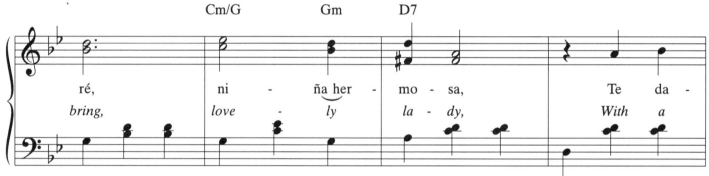

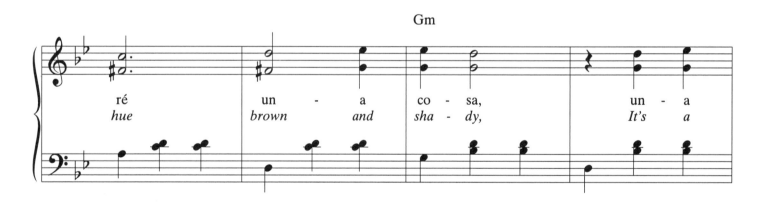

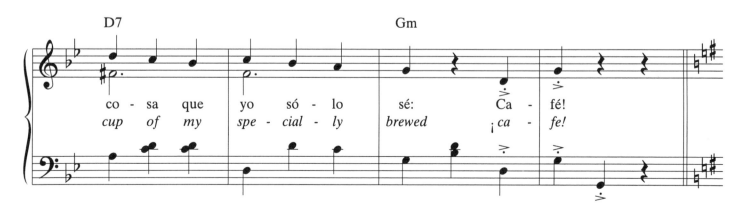

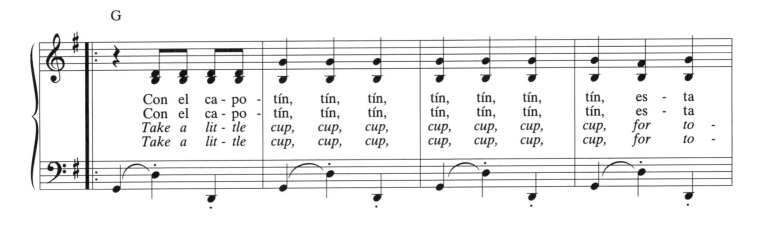

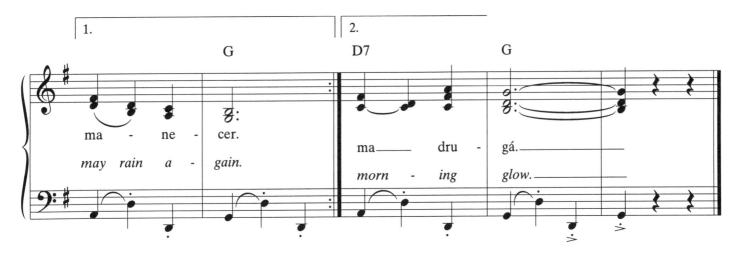

ATF121

El capotín

(Song on page 68)

Making Up New Verses

This happy folk song from Puerto Rico is full of talk about the weather. Can you make up some new verses about the weather? For example, ... *this evening they say it may hail ... in the morning we'll go for a sail.* Or how about *for tonight they're expecting some wind ... when it blows it will make the tree bend.* What other kinds of weather can you think of? Storms, tornadoes, sleet? There are so many different kinds of weather. Use your imagination to think up new verses about the weather.

If you would like to sing this song the way children do in Puerto Rico here is they way the words will sound.

Yo te daré, te daré, niña hermosa,
Joh teh dah-reh, teh dah-reh neen-yah ehr-moh-sah,

Te daré una cosa,
Teh dah-reh oo-nah koh-sah,

Una cosa que yo sólo sé: ¡Café!
Oo-nah koh-sah keh joh soh-loh seh: kah-feh!

Con el capotín, tín, tín, tín, tín, tín, tín,
Kohn ehl kah-poh-teen, teen, teen, teen, teen, teen, teen,

esta noche va a llover.
ehs-tah noh-cheh vah ah joh-behr.

Con el capotín, tín, tín, tín, tín, tín, tín,
Kohn ehl kah-poh-teen, teen, teen, teen, teen, teen,

a eso del amanecer.
ah eh-soh dehl ah-mah-neh-sehr.

Con el capotín . . .
Kohn ehl kah-poh-teen . . .

esta noche va a nevar.
eh s-tah noh-cheh vah ah neh-bahr.
Con el capotín . . .
Kohn ehl kah-poh-teen . . .

a eso de la madrugá.
ah eh-soh deh lah mah-droo-gah.

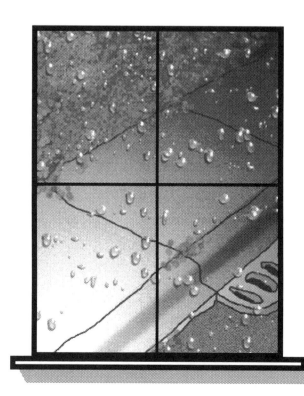

Over the River and Through the Woods

**Words and Music by
Lydia Maria Child**

Our Animal Friends

Pussy Cat, Pussy Cat

Traditional English

Copyright © 1998 by Carl Fischer, Inc.

Hey, Diddle, Diddle

Traditional English

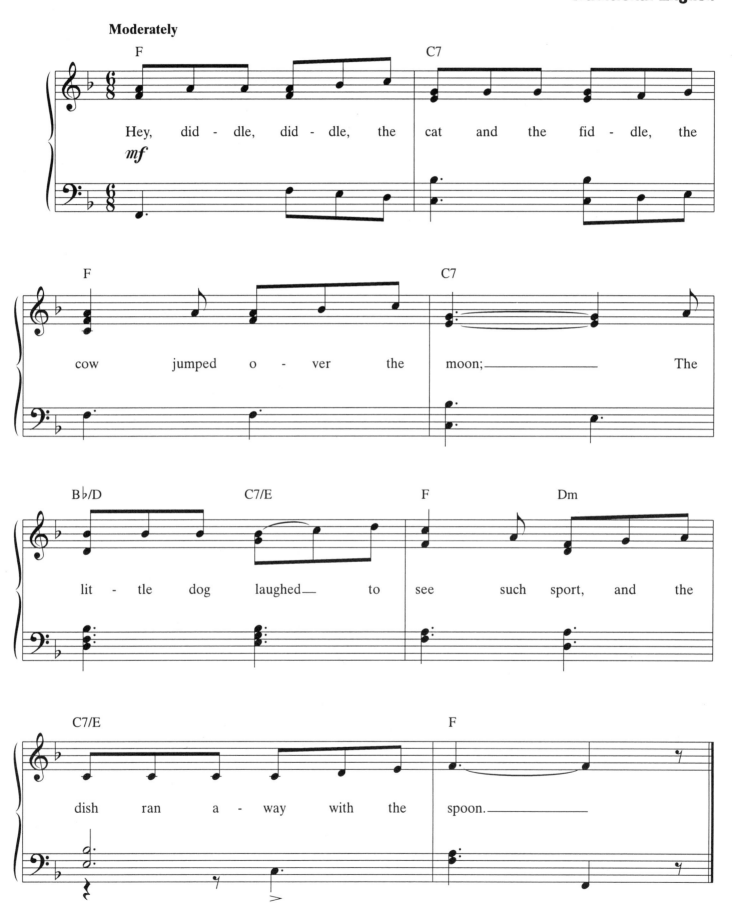

Moderately

Hey, did-dle, did-dle, the cat and the fid-dle, the cow jumped o-ver the moon;_____ The lit-tle dog laughed__ to see such sport, and the dish ran a-way with the spoon._____

Hey, Diddle, Diddle

Drawing a Picture

You've probably sung this song many times. It's fun to draw a picture to show what's happening in the song. You can make several pictures to show the action in each line — for example, a picture of the cat playing a fiddle, then a picture of the cow jumping over the moon, and so forth. Or you can make one picture of all these things happening at once. Use a large sheet of paper to make your drawing so you'll have plenty of room. When you've finished, show your parents or teacher what you've drawn. They might want to hang it up somewhere to show everyone else. You might even want to hang it in your room for all your friends to see.

If you have made several pictures, one of each event in the song, try mixing them up and then putting them in the right order. Or hang them up *out of* order and then point to each one *in* order as you sing the song for your parents, friends, or teacher.

You can use your eraser to make pictures too! Make a scribbled background using the side of a lead pencil. Then, using an eraser, erase the "scribbling."

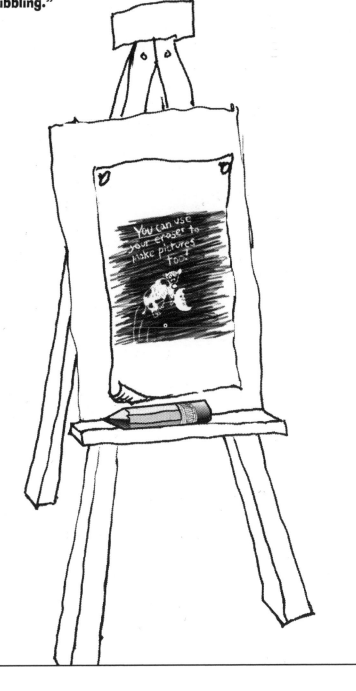

The Dog and the Cat

Traditional English

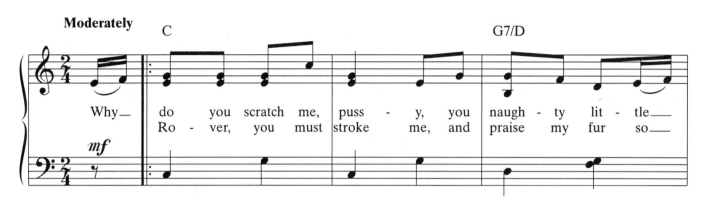

Why— do you scratch me, puss - y, you naugh - ty lit - tle—
Ro - ver, you must stroke me, and praise my fur so—

thing? Un - less you stop, Miss Puss - y, an -
white! Must— pet me and ca - ress— me for—

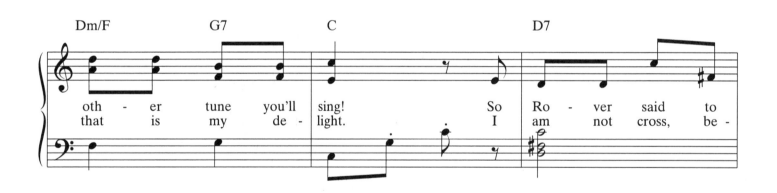

oth - er tune you'll sing! So Ro - ver said to
that is my de - light. I am not cross, to be -

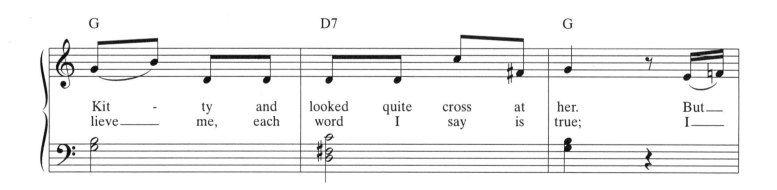

Kit - ty and looked quite cross at her. But—
lieve— me, and each word I say is true; I—

3. But Rover said to kitty, there is no truth in that,
Although you purr so gently, one can't believe a cat.
I'm grieved to say, Miss Pussy, you I can never trust!
I know your claws are cruel, and run away I must.
Bow-wow, bow-wow, bow-wow, bow-wow, now run away I must;
Bow-wow, bow-wow, bow-wow, bow-wow, now run away I must.

La cucaracha

English Lyric by David Eddleman

Mexican Folk Song

Brightly

Una cu-ca-ra-cha pin-ta, Le di-jo a una co-lo-ra-da,
Lit-tle bug who's out a-sun-ning, Chase it off and set it run-ning;

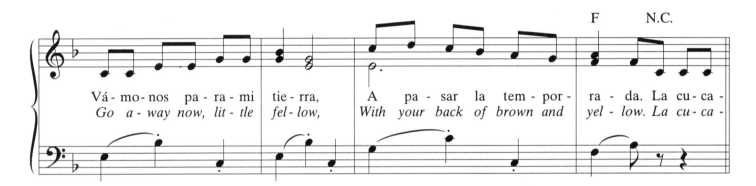

Vá-mo-nos pa-ra-mi tie-rra, A pa-sar la tem-por-ra-da. La cu-ca-
Go a-way now, lit-tle fel-low, With your back of brown and yel-low. La cu-ca-

ra-cha, la cu-ca-ra-cha, Ya no quie-re ca-mi-nar, Por-que no
ra-cha, la cu-ca-ra-cha, I know you don't want to go. But you've no

tie-ne, por-que le fal-ta, Di-ne-ro pa-ra gas-tar.
mon-ey to buy your sup-per, Oh, how sad, your tale of woe.

La cucaracha

Sing in Spanish

In Spanish, *la cucaracha* means *the cockroach.* There are a lot of stories told to explain where this song came from in Mexico. Some say it isn't about an insect at all, that "cockroach" is a nickname for "a little dancer." Others say it is a nickname for a politician! Whatever it means, it is one of the most popular songs in Mexico and it's fun to sing it in Spanish. Here is how the words are pronounced in Mexico.

Una cucaracha pinta,
Oo-nah koo-kah-rah-chah peen-tah,

Le dijo_a_una colorada,
Leh dee-hoh_ah_oo-nah koh-loh-rah-dah,

Vámonos para mi tierra,
Bah-moh-nos pah-rah mee tyeh-rrah,

A pasar la temporada.
Ah pah-sahr lah tehm-poh-rah-dah.

La cucaracha, la cucaracha,
Lah koo-kah-rah-chah, lah koo-kah-rah-chah,

Ya no quiere caminar,
Yah noh kyeh-reh kah-mee-nahr,

Porque no tiene, porque le falta,
Pohr-keh noh tyeh-neh, pohr-keh leh fahl-tah,

Dinero para gastar.
Dee-neh-roh pah-rah gahs-tahr.

A Frog He Would A-Courtin' Go

American Folk Song

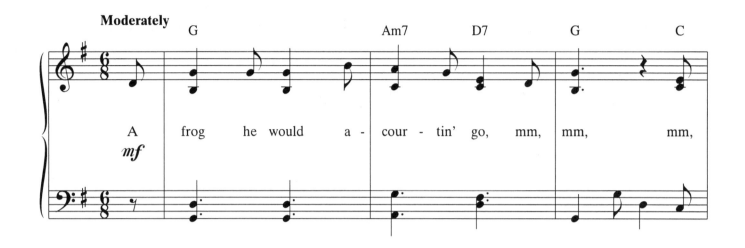

A frog he would a-cour-tin' go, mm, mm, mm,

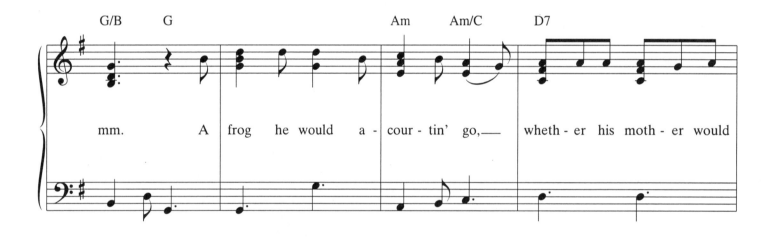

mm. A frog he would a-cour-tin' go,— wheth-er his moth-er would

let him or, no, mm, mm, mm, mm.

Copyright © 1998 by Carl Fischer, Inc.

2. He rode right to Miss Mousie's den, m, m, m, m.
   He rode right to Miss Mousie's den,
   Said he, "Miss Mousie are you within?" m, m, m, m.

3. "Oh, yes kind sir, I sit and spin,
   Oh, yes kind sir, I sit and spin,
   Lift the latch and walk right in."

4. He said, "Miss Mouse I've come to see,"
   He said, "Miss Mouse I've come to see?
   If you, Miss Mousie, will marry me?"

5. Oh, as for that I cannot say,
   Oh, as for that I cannot say,
   For Mister Mousie has gone away.

6. A fine young gentelmen has been here,...
   A fine young gentelmen has been here,...
   Who wants to marry me, it is clear,...

7. Mister Mousie gave his consent,
   Mister Mousie gave his consent,
   And the weasel wrote the publishment.

8. Where shall the wedding supper be?
   Where shall the wedding supper be?
   Way down yonder in a hollow tree.

9. The first that came was a bumble bee,
   The first that came was a bumble bee,
   Carrying a fiddle on his knee.

10. The next that came was a big black bug,
    The next that came was a big black bug,
    On his back was a water jug.

11. Bread and butter lie on the shelf,
    Bread and butter lie on the shelf,
    If you want more then sing it yourself.

Old MacDonald Had a Farm

American Folk Song

2. Old MacDonald had a farm, E-I-E-I-O!
And on his farm he had some cows, E-I-E-I-O!
With a moo moo here and a moo moo there,
Here a moo, there a moo, everywhere a moo moo.
Old MacDonald had a farm, E-I-E-I-O!

3. ... And on his farm he had some pigs,...
With an oink oink here...

4. ... And on his farm he had some ducks,...
With a quack quack here...

5. ... And on his farm he had some crows,...
With a caw caw here...

Old Macdonald Had a Farm

E

Play the Recorder

This part to play with "Old Macdonald" uses not only G, A, and B, but a new note — E — as well. You may have played it before, if not at school then maybe with one of the songs in this book. If you can't remember the fingering, or don't know it, here it is —

Practice this part and then play it as your family or friends sing the song.

All Around the Kitchen

African American Play Song
Transcribed from
Library Of Congress Field
Recording AFS 88

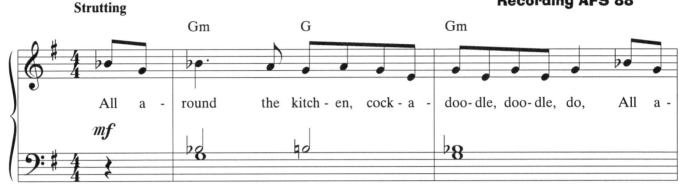

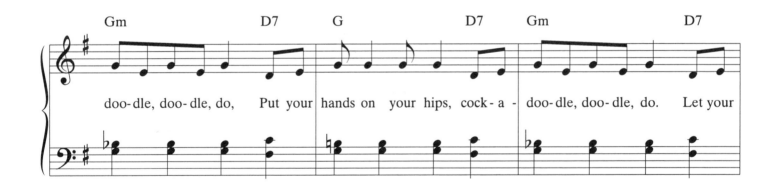

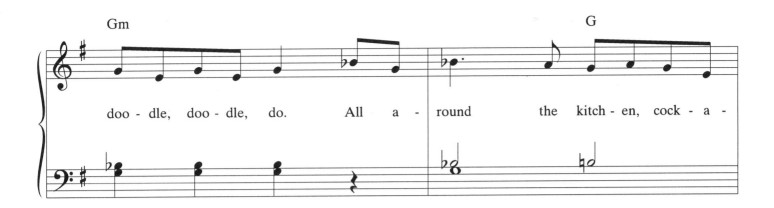

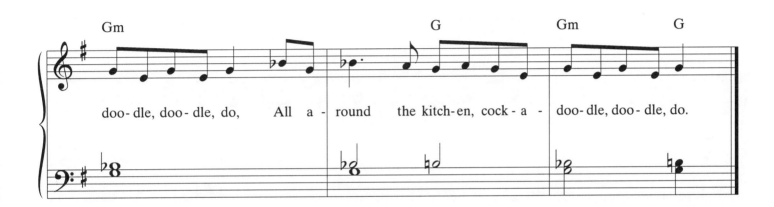

All Around the Kitchen

Follow the Leader

Here's an action song that's lots of fun to do. When you get to the following words in the song, do the actions that the words tell you to do:

All around the kitchen — Strut "around the kitchen" the way a rooster would.
Now stop right still — Stop in place with your arms to your sides.
Put your hands on your hips — Place your hands on your hips.
Let your right foot slip — With your right foot, keep your heel in place and move your toes
                       from side to side.
Then do it like this — Still with hands on hips, rock your body from side to side.
All around the kitchen — Once more strut "around the kitchen" like a rooster.

Camptown Races

**Words and Music by
Stephen Foster**

Copyright © 1998 by Carl Fischer, Inc.

Camptown Races

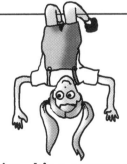

Playing a Doodah

This song is by Stephen Foster. You will find another of Mr. Foster's songs in this book. It's called "Oh, Susanna" and it's on page 110.

"Camptown Races" has a word that repeats — *doodah*. It doesn't mean anything. It's a nonsense word, a little like singing *fa la la la la*. Find a drum and whenever you come to the word *doodah* or *oh, doodah day*, play the rhythm of the words instead of singing them. This is fun to do with your friends. Your friends can sing the song and you can join in playing the *doodahs* and *oh, doodah days* on your drum.

Goodby, Old Paint

American Cowboy Song

Moderately

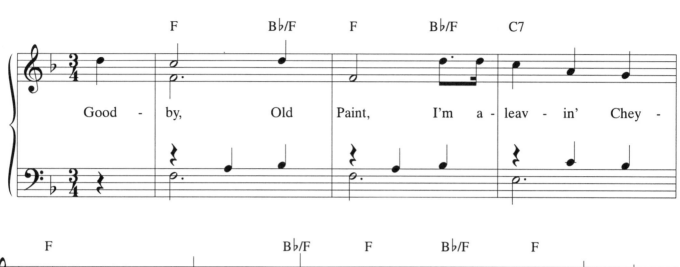

Good - by, Old Paint, I'm a - leav - in' Chey -

enne. Good - by, Old Paint, I'm a - leav - in' Chey -

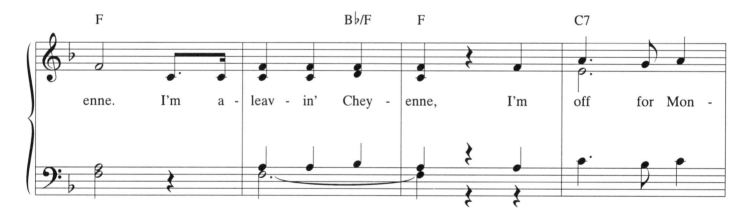

enne. I'm a - leav - in' Chey - enne, I'm off for Mon -

tan', Good - by, Old Paint, I'm a - leav - in' Chey - enne.

Pop! Goes the Weasel

Traditional English

ATF121

Three Blind Mice

Traditional Round

Three Blind Mice

A Marching Round

Older children can perform "Three Blind Mice" as a round. The entrances for each voice are marked in the music.

Form a line behind a leader. As you march to "Three Blind Mice" the leader makes up a movement to do in the first line (*Three blind mice . . .*). In the second line (*See how they run . . .*) everyone behind the leader imitates the leader's movement, but the leader now makes up a new movement for everyone to imitate. This continues throughout the song. At the end of the song the leader goes to the rear of the line. The next person in line becomes the leader and makes up new movements.

Pony Boy

Traditional American

Po - ny boy, po - ny boy, won't you be my po - ny boy?

Ride 'em high, ride 'em low, ride 'em cross the plain.

Mar - ry me, car - ry me, won't you, po - ny boy? Gid - dy

up, gid - dy up, gid - dy up! Whoa! My po - ny boy.

Pony Boy

Ride Like a Cowboy

With a group of friends form a circle. Use a broom and ride it as if you're riding a horse. (The broom part, of course, will be the horse's head.) The rider is the Pony Boy or Pony Girl.

1. As the circle people sing they walk to their left.
2. The rider gallops along inside the circle — in the opposite direction — beginning with the first words, *Pony boy* (or *Pony girl* if a girl is riding).
3. At the words *Marry me*, get off and "walk the horse."
4. Then, at the words *Giddy up*, gallop on the horse again until the word *Whoa!*
5. At the word *Whoa!* everyone stops, the children in the circle face the center, and the rider faces the person he or she has stopped in front of.
6. As the circle finishes the song, the rider gets off the "horse" and gives it to that person. That child becomes the new Pony Boy or Pony Girl.

The game continues until everyone has had a chance to be Pony Boy or Pony Girl.

My Pony

Traditional Children's Song

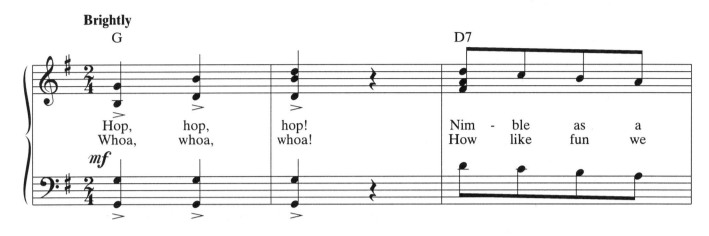

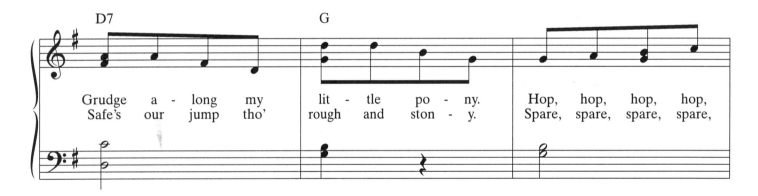

My Pony

Play the Recorder

Practice this part on your recorder to play with "My Pony." The only notes it uses are **G, A,** and **B.**
The rhythm is not hard either. It uses only quarter notes ♩ and eighth notes ♫. You know that
eighth notes go twice as fast as quarter notes. Say the words, *going to the fairground.* If you wrote
that out using quarter notes and eighth notes it would look like this —

Now play this recorder part as others sing.

Mister Rabbit

African American Play Song

3. "Your coat's mighty gray."
   "Yes, indeed, 'twas made that way."

4. "Your tail's mighty white."
   "Yes, indeed, I'm going out o' sight."

Mister Rabbit

Making Up New Words

Mister Rabbit has some very funny replies to the comments about his ears, foot, coat, and tail. Try making up some new rhymes about Mister Rabbit. For example,

> *Your foot's like a cat!*
> *Yes, indeed, I like it like that.*
> or
> *Your leg's mighty short!*
> *Yes, indeed, it's good for sport.*

Now can you make up some rhymes about Mister Rabbit's teeth? His fur? His toes? His eyes?

John the Rabbit

African American Game Song

Copyright © 1998 by Carl Fischer, Inc.

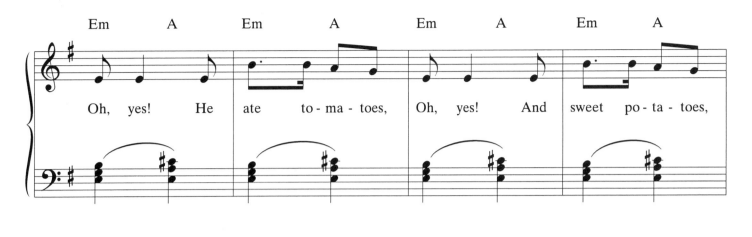

Em A Em A Em A Em A

Oh, yes! He ate to-ma-toes, Oh, yes! And sweet po-ta-toes,

Em A E A E A E A E

Oh, yes! And if I live, Oh, yes! To see next fall,

A E A E A E B7 E

Oh, yes! I won't have, Oh, yes! A gar-den at all!

John the Rabbit

Play a Refrain

After each line of "John the Rabbit" you sing the words *oh, yes.* Try singing the song using a drum or clapping on the words *oh, yes* instead of singing them. The note for the words *oh, yes* is an E. You can play that on your recorder. If you don't remember the fingering here it is.

Play the *oh, yes* part on the recorder E as others sing.

Who Built the Ark?

African American Spiritual

2. (He) built it long, both wide and tall,
   Plenty of room for the large and small.

3. Now in come the animals two by two,
   Hippopotamus and kangaroo,

4. Now in come animals three by three,
   The big cats and a bumblebee. *Refrain*

5. Now in come the animals four by four,
   Two by the window and two by the door,

6. Now in come the animals five by five,
   Four little wrens and the robin's wife,

7. Now in come the animals six by six,
   Elephant laughed at the monkey's tricks,

8. Now in come the animals seven by seven,
   Four from home and three from heaven.
   Refrain

9. Now in come animals eight by eight,
   Some on time and the others late,

10. Now in come animals nine by nine,
    Some was a-shouting and some was a-crying.

11. Now in come the animals ten by ten,
    Five black roosters and five black hens,

12. Now Noah says, "Go shut that door,
    The rain's started dropping and we can't
    take more." *Refrain*

Who Built the Ark?

Making Puppets

Find or draw pictures of the animals named in the song — hippopotamus,
kangaroo, cat, bumblebee, wren, robin, elephant, monkey, rooster, hen. You can choose others as
well for the verses that don't mention a special animal.

1. Paste the pictures on a sheet of thin cardboard, like a shirt cardboard.
2. When the paste is dry, cut out the animal picture and attach a long, thin stick — like a tongue
   depressor or an ice cream stick — to the back. If you use empty cardboard tubes from bathroom
   tissue rolls, you can control the puppet by sticking your fingers inside the roll.
3. Now present a puppet show to your friends, parents, or classmates. You can crouch behind a sofa
   or table and use the top as a stage.
4. As you sing the song, have the animal move from one side of the "stage" to the other.

If you have several puppeteers you can present several animals at one time for a grand finale. If you
like, you can put a number on each animal to go with the numbers in the verses.

Three Little Kittens

Nursery Rhyme Song

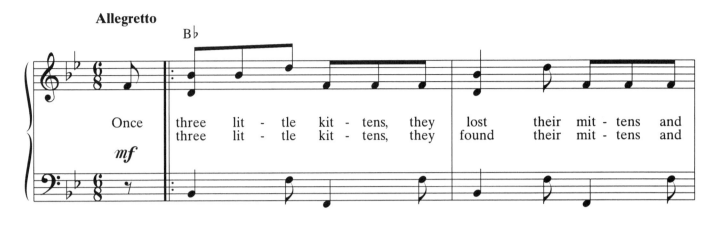

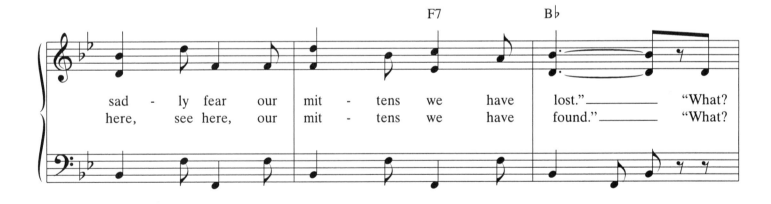

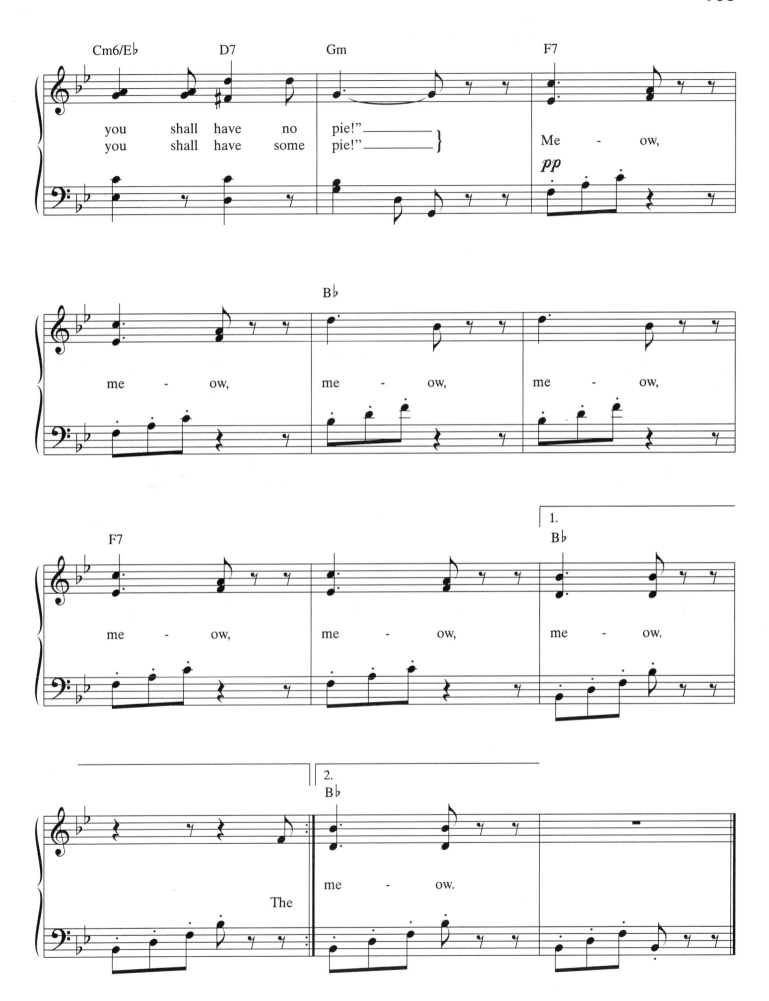

Where Has My Little Dog Gone?

**Words and Music by
Septimus Winner**

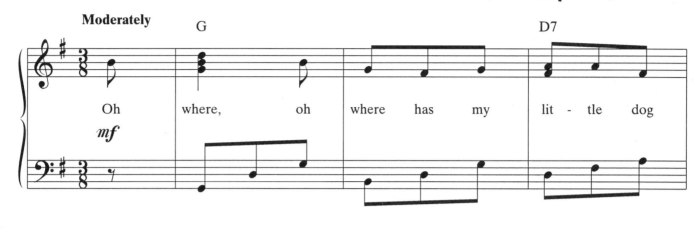

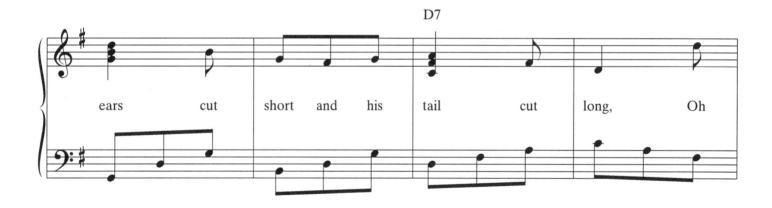

Where Has My Little Dog Gone?

Play the Recorder

This part to play on the recorder with "Where Has My Little Dog Gone?" uses only the notes G, A, and B. This is a simple part that you should pick up very quickly. Be careful not to start playing on that eighth rest at the beginning. Your first note should fall on the word *where*.

Bingo

American Folk Song

*replace letter with hand clap.

4. _ _ _ G - O
5. _ _ _ _ - O
6. _ _ _ _ - _

Bingo

Filling Up the Silences

When you sing "Bingo" all the way through you drop a letter from Bingo's name each time you sing a verse until you don't sing any letters at all. You have to hear the letters in your mind to know when to start singing again. Sometimes it helps to make a movement during the silent letters. Try singing the song, but when you leave out a letter, tap your ear or make a "chug" movement with your arm (like a YES! movement) in place of the letter. For example, you would tap *(TAP)*-I-N-GO, then *(TAP)*-*(TAP)*-N-G-O, and so on. Use your imagination to think of other movements you can do.

There's a Hole in the Bucket

American Folk Song

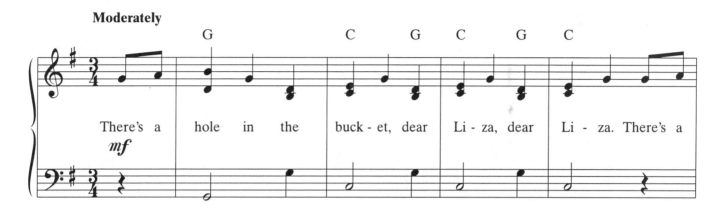

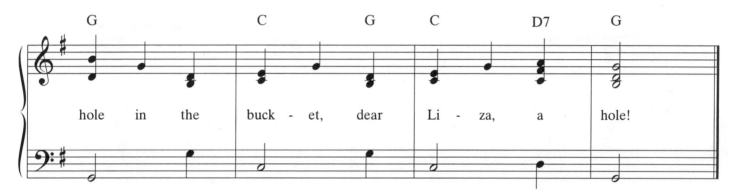

2. Well, fix it, dear Henry,...
3. With what shall I fix it, dear Liza,...
4. With a straw, dear Henry,...
5. But the straw is too long, dear Liza,...
6. Then cut it, dear Henry,...
7. With what shall I cut it, dear Liza,...
8. With a knife, dear Henry,...
9. But the knife is too dull, dear Liza,...
10. Then sharpen it, dear Henry,...

11. With what shall I sharpen it, dear Liza,...
12. With a stone, dear Henry,...
13. But the stone is too dry, dear Liza,...
14. Then wet it, dear Henry,...
15. With what shall I wet it, dear Liza,...
16. With water, dear Henry,...
17. In what shall I carry it, dear Liza,...
18. In a bucket, dear Henry,...
19. There's a hole in the bucket, dear Liza,...

There's a Hole in the Bucket

E

Play the Recorder

You can play this recorder part with "There's a Hole in the Bucket" as others sing. You will need your old friends — G, A, and B — and a new note, E. It is fingered like this —

Make sure you don't play on the quarter rest. Your first note falls on the word *hole*.

Oh, Susanna

**Words and Music by
Stephen Foster**

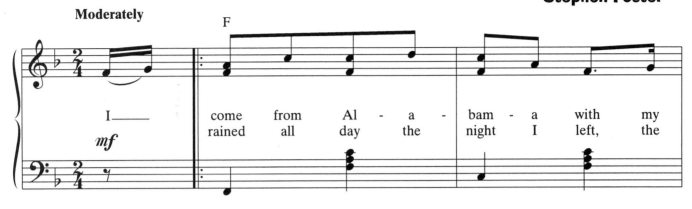

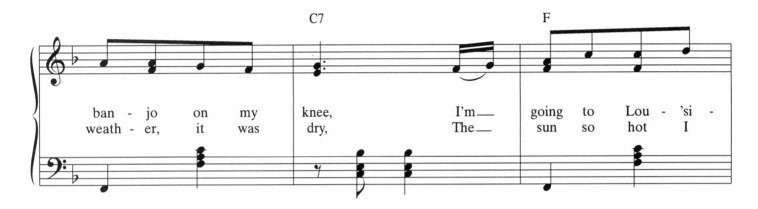

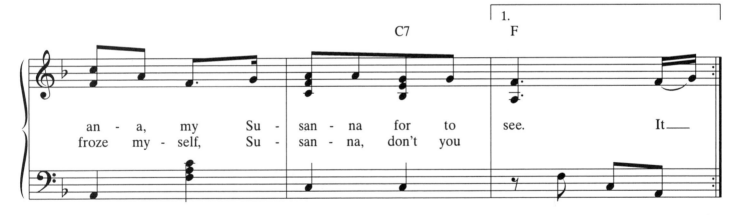

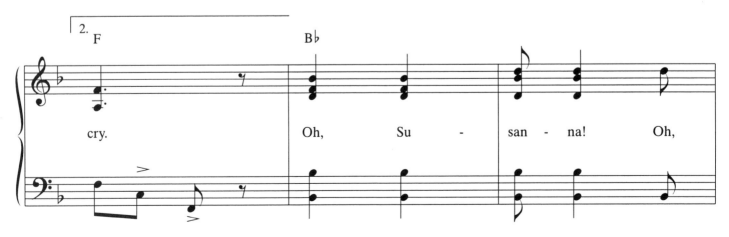

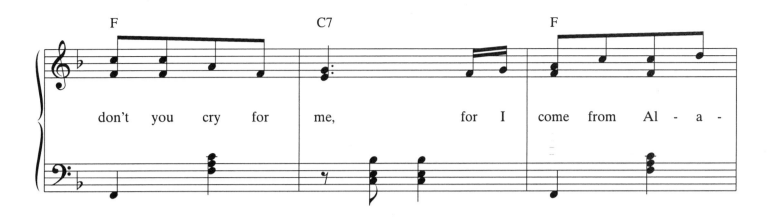

don't you cry for me,   for I come from Al - a -

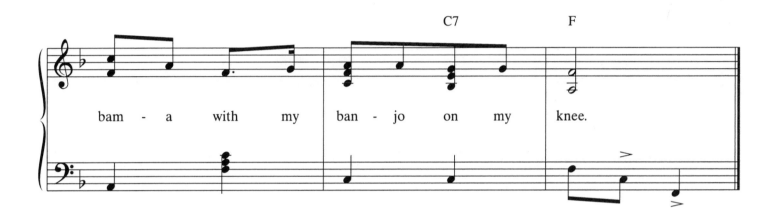

bam - a with my ban - jo on my knee.

Oh, Susanna

Looking It Up

Stephen Foster was America's first great writer of popular songs. Although he died over 130 years ago, we still sing his songs—songs like "Jeanie with the Light Brown Hair" and "Old Folks at Home." Go to the library and ask the librarian to help you find out something about Stephen Foster. He did not have a very happy life. When you've learned all you can about Mr. Foster, tell your parents, teachers, or classmates about him. There is another song by Mr. Foster in this book. It's called "Camptown Races" and it's on pg. 86.

This Old Man

Traditional English

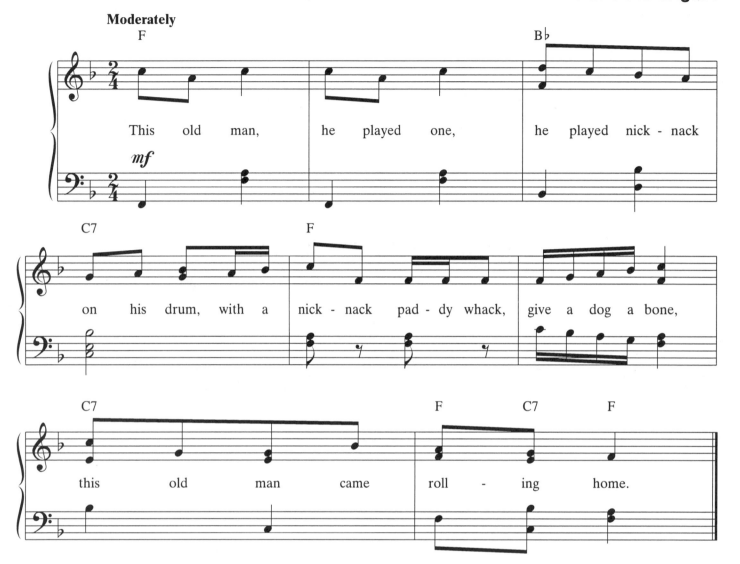

two... on his shoe,

three... on the tree,

four... on the door,

five... on the hive,

six... on the sticks,

seven... up in heaven,

eight... on the gate,

nine... on the line,

ten... once again,

Copyright © 1998 by Carl Fischer, Inc.

This Old Man

A Game with Ten Pencils

Find ten pencils or other small objects that are alike (like marbles, checkers, or jacks). As you sing "This Old Man" lay a pencil down in front of you on the first verse. Add another pencil on each verse until you have ten pencils lying in front of you. To add some extra fun, sing the song in reverse order, starting with verse 10, then verse 9, then verse 8, and so forth. As you sing the verses in reverse order, pick up a pencil at the beginning of each verse. By the time you get back to verse 1 you should have only one pencil lying in front of you. Pick it up and draw a picture of the old man rolling home.

If you have ten children you can all crouch in a circle. At each number children jump up and then return to the crouch. For example, on *one*, one child jumps up and returns to the crouch. On *two*, that child and the person next to him or her jumps up and returns to the crouch, continuing until all ten children jump up on the word *ten*. Then you can reverse the pattern by singing the verses of the song in reverse order. Fun!

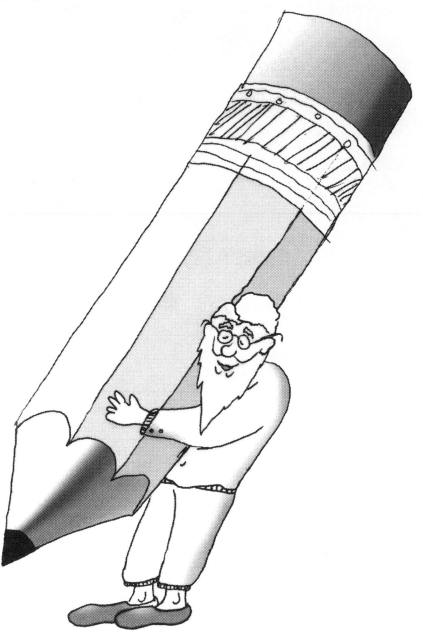

Lullabies

Now the Day Is Over

**Hymn Composed by
Joseph Barnby**

Moderately slow

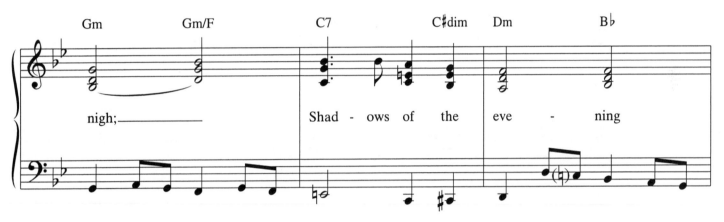

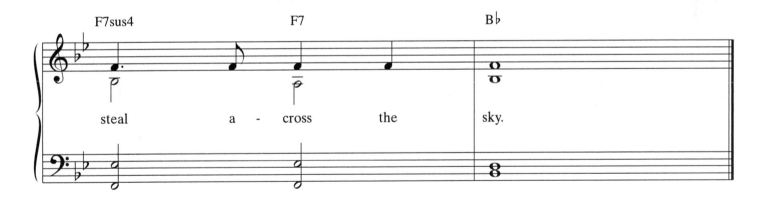

2. Now the darkness gathers, stars begin to peep;
   Birds and beasts and flowers soon will be asleep.

Rock-a-bye, Baby

**Composed by
Effie I. Canning (1884)**

Rock-a-Bye, Baby

Sing Loud or Sing Soft?

"Rock-a-Bye, Baby" is a lullaby. Do you know what a lullaby is? It's a song meant to help a baby go to sleep. Do you think you would sing a lullaby softly or loudly? Sing "Rock-a-Bye, Baby" in a loud voice. Do you think the baby will go to sleep if you sing that way? Now sing "Rock-a-Bye, Baby" in a soft voice. Do you think singing with a soft voice is a better way to help the baby go to sleep?

Try singing in a loud or soft voice with other songs in this book. Which do you think is a better way to sing the songs you choose?

Twinkle, Twinkle, Little Star

Traditional English

Copyright © 1998 by Carl Fischer, Inc.

Twinkle, Twinkle, Little Star

LISTENING TO MUSIC

After you have learned this song, find a recording of a piece by W. A. Mozart called *Variations on "Ah, vous dirai-je, Maman"*. Your parents or your music teacher can help you find it. The recording may even be in your town or school library's audio section. Play the recording. You will hear something familiar. Mr. Mozart used a version of "Twinkle, Twinkle, Little Star" to write his piece. And as the piece goes on you still hear the melody, but Mozart changes it each time it's played. When you change a melody it's called a *variation*. Mozart loved to write variations on simple melodies. This piece is just one of them!

Chippewa Lullaby

Chippewa Folk Song

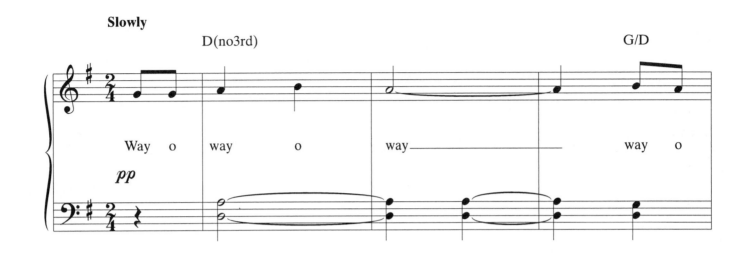

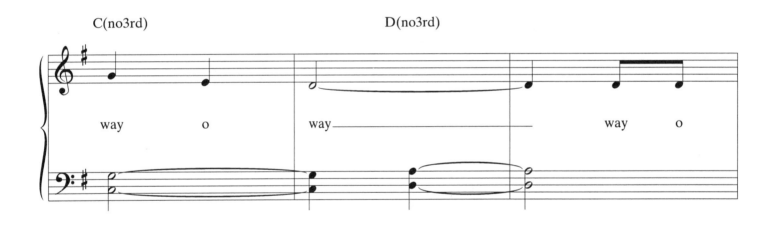

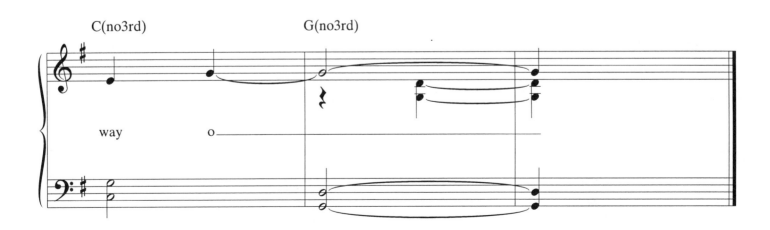

The Child And The Star

Traditional

Go To Sleep, Lena Darling

Words and Music by Dan Emmett

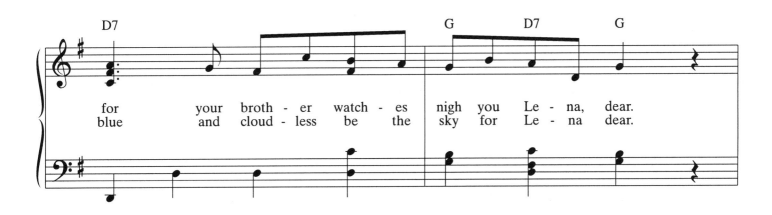

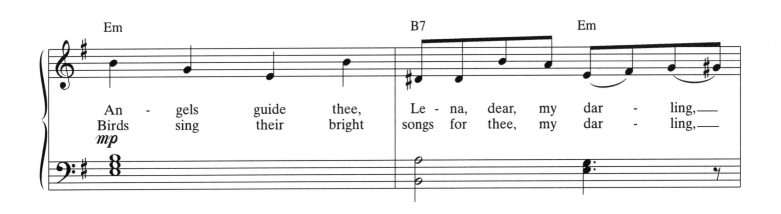

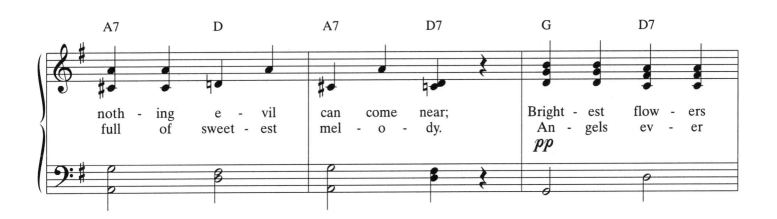

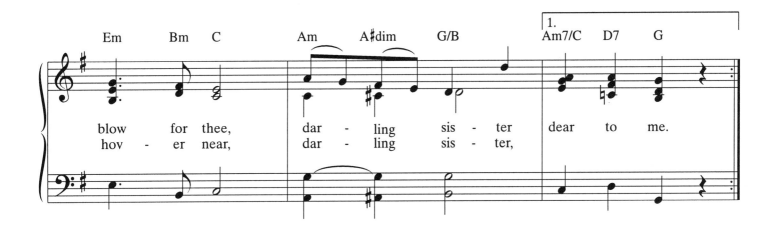

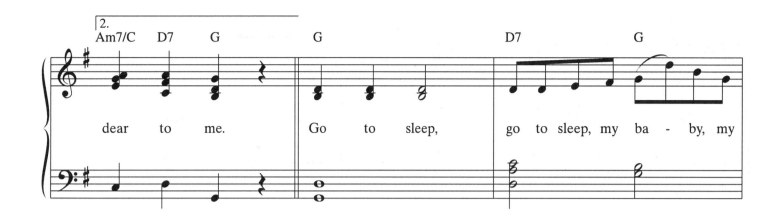

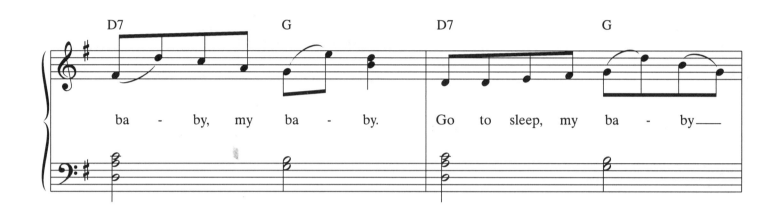

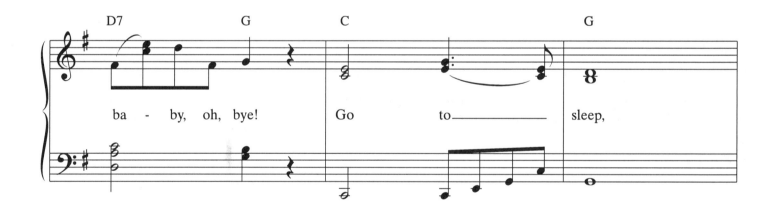

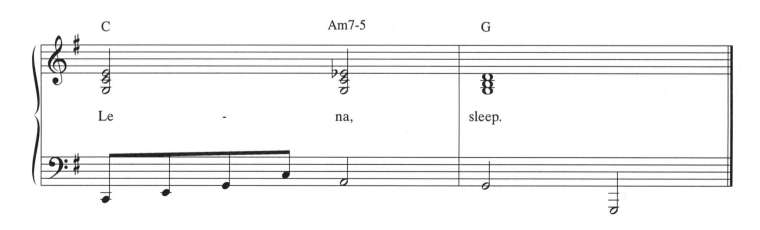

Songs
from
Our Heritage

Row, Row, Row Your Boat

Traditional English Round

Row, Row, Row Your Boat

Follow the Leader

Older children can sing "Row, Row, Row Your Boat" as a round. The second voice starts singing when the first voice sings *Merrily, merrily, merrily, merrily.*

You can also do a follow-the-leader game with this song.
1. With some friends, form a line or group behind or around a leader. Decide how many times you will sing the song as a round.
2. The leader makes up a movement to do in the first line (it might be a rowing movement).
3. In the second line the "followers" repeat the movement that the leader has done, while the leader goes on to make up another movement.
4. In the third line the "followers" repeat the leader's new movement while the leader goes on to make up another, and so on throughout the song.
5. At the end the leader joins the group and the next person becomes the leader. (Everyone can clap their hands four times to show the song has ended.)

The game ends when everyone has had a chance to be the leader.

Streets of Laredo

American Cowboy Song

Lyrics under the music:

As I ____ walked out in the streets of La - re - do, As I walked out in La - re do one day, I spied a young cow - boy wrapped up in white lin - en, wrapped up in white lin - en and cold as the clay.

2. "I see by your outfit that you are a cowboy,"
   These words he said as I boldly walked by;
   "Come listen to me and I'll tell my sad story:
   I'm shot in the chest and I'm sure I will die."

3. "Now once in the saddle I used to ride handsome,
   'A handsome young cowboy' is what they would say,
   I'd ride into town and go down to the cardhouse,
   But I'm shot in the chest and I'm dying today."

4. "Go run to the spring for a cup of cold water,
   To cool down my fever," the young cowboy said.
   But when I returned, his poor soul had departed,
   And I wept when I saw the young cowboy was dead.

5. We'll bang the drum slowly and play the fife lowly,
   We'll play the dead march as we bear him along.
   We'll go to the graveyard and lay the sod o'er him;
   He was a young cowboy, but he had done wrong.

La borinqueña

Words by Manuel Fernández Juncos
English Lyric by Kathleen Bernath

Music by Félix Astol Artés

Copyright © 1998 by Carl Fischer, Inc.

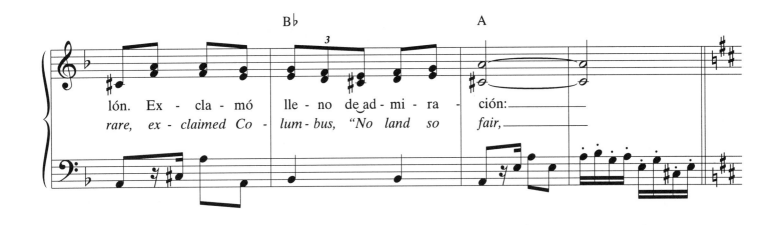

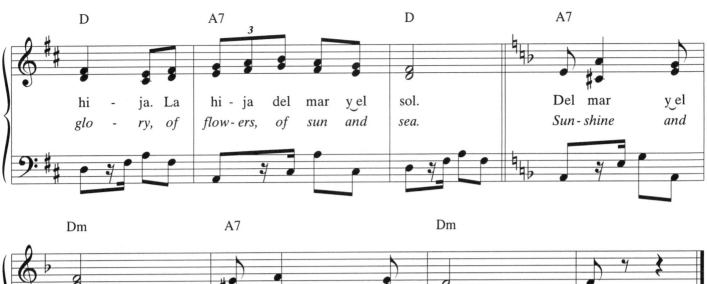

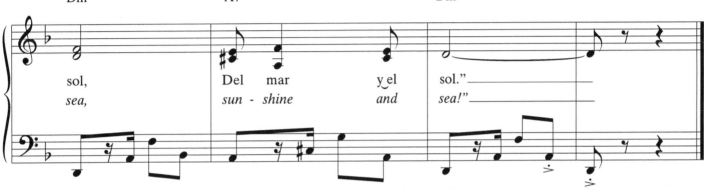

La borinqueña

Sing in Spanish

"La borinqueña" (pronounced *lah bohr-een-KEHN-yah*) is considered the national anthem of Puerto Rico. Borinquen is the name that the original people of Puerto Rico, the Taino Indians, gave to their island. You can sing the beautiful Spanish words, too, if you know the pronunciation. This is how you say and sing the Spanish in Puerto Rico.

La tierra de Borinquen,
Lah tyehr-rah deh Bohr-een-kehn,

Donde he nacido yo,
Dohn-deh eh nah-see-doh joh,

Es un jardín florido
Ehs oon har-deen floh-ree-doh

De mágico primor.
Deh mah-hee-koh pree-mohr.

Un cielo siempre nítido
Oon syeh-loh syehm-preh nee-tee-doh

Le sirve de dosel.
Leh seer-beh deh doh-sehl.

Y dan arrullo plácido
Ee dahn ah-rroo-joh plah-see-doh

Las olas a sus pies.
Lahs oh-las ah soos pyehs.

Cuando a sus playas vino Colón,
Kwahn-doh ah soos plah-yas bee-noh Koh-lohn,

Exclamó lleno de admiración:
Ehs-klah-moh jeh-noh deh ahd-mee-rah-syohn:

"Esta es la linda tierra
"Ehs-tah ehs lah leen-dah tye-rrah

Que busco yo;
Keh boos-koh joh;

Es Borinquen la hija,
Ehs Boh-reen-kehn lah ee-hah,

La hija del mar y el sol,
Lah ee-hah dehl mahr ee ehl sohl,

Del mar y el sol,
Dehl mahr ee ehl sohl,

Del mar y el sol."
Dehl mahr ee ehl sohl."

My Grandfather's Clock

(Activity on page 134)

Words and Music by
Henry Clay Work

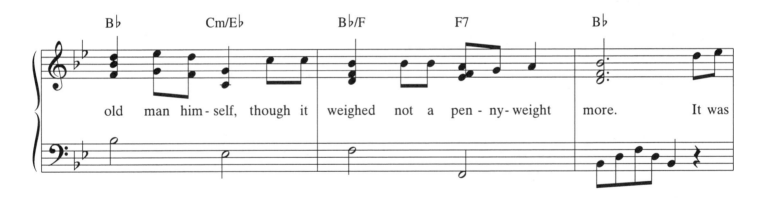

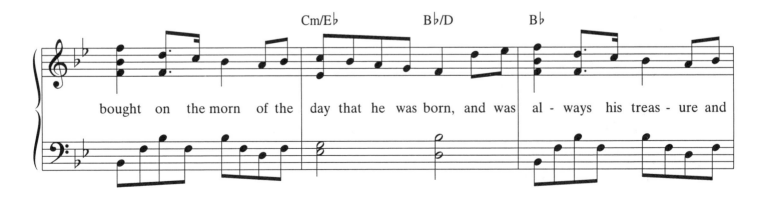

2. In watching its pendulum swing to and fro,
   Many hours had he spent while a boy;
   And in childhood and manhood the clock seemed to know
   And to share both his grief and his joy.
   For it struck twenty-four when he entered the door,
   With a blooming and beautiful bride.
   But it stopped...

3. My grandfather said that of those he could hire,
   Not a servant so faithful he found;
   For it wasted no time and had but one desire
   At the close of each week to be wound.
   And it kept in its place, not a frown upon its face,
   And its hands never hung by its side.
   But it stopped...

My Grandfather's Clock

Ticking and Tocking

You can make "tick-tocks" to go with "My Grandfather's Clock." Have you ever made clicks with your tongue? Place the tip of the tongue against the roof of your mouth so that the back is entirely closed off. Then pull your tongue back until it falls into the bottom of your mouth, making a loud "click" that can sound like the tick-tock of a large clock, like a Grandfather's clock. Once you have the hang of it, do your tongue tick-tocks with the song. You can sing while others make the tick-tocks, or you can make them yourself while others sing. Try singing everything by yourself. Sing the song all the way through until you get to the words *tick, tock, tick, tock*. Then, instead of singing those words, do your tick-tocks with your tongue instead.

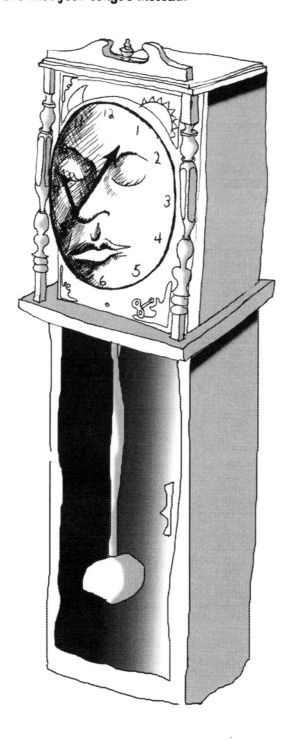

Clementine

American Miner's Song

Moderately

VERSE

1. In a cav-ern, in a can-yon, Ex-ca-vat-ing for a mine, Dwelt a

min-er, for-ty nin-er, And his daugh-ter Clem-en-tine. Oh, my

REFRAIN

dar-ling, oh, my dar-ling, Oh, my dar-ling Clem-en-tine, You are

lost and gone for-ev-er, Dread-ful sor-ry, Clem-en-tine.

2. Light she was and like a fairy,
   And her shoes were number nine,
   Herring boxes without topses,
   Sandals were for Clementine.
   (Refrain)

3. Drove she ducklings to the water
   Every morning just at nine,
   Hit her foot against a splinter,
   Fell into the foaming brine.
   (Refrain)

4. Ruby lips above the water
   Blowing bubbles soft and fine,
   But, alas, I was no swimmer,
   So I lost my Clementine.
   (Refrain)

Cielito lindo

English Lyrics by David Eddleman

Mexican Folk Song

Gaily

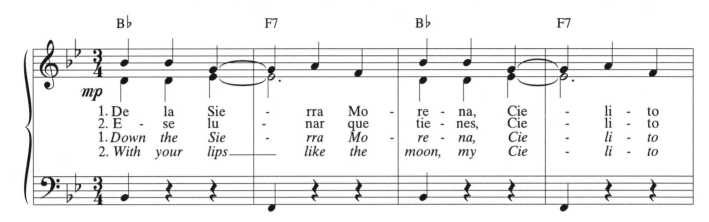

1. De la Sie - rra Mo - re - na, Cie - li - to
2. E - se lu - nar que tie - nes, Cie - li - to
1. *Down the Sie - rra Mo - re - na, Cie - li - to*
2. *With your lips like the moon, my Cie - li - to*

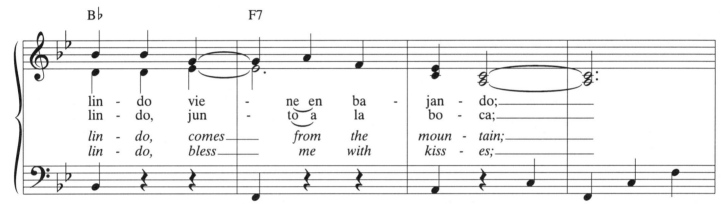

lin - do vie - ne en ba - jan - do;
lin - do, jun - to a la bo - ca;
lin - do, comes from the moun - tain;
lin - do, bless me with kiss - es;

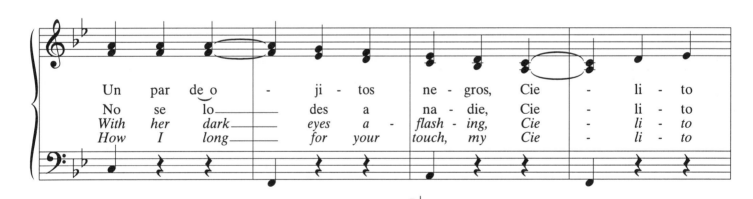

Un par de o - ji - tos ne - gros, Cie - li - to
No se lo des a na - die, Cie - li - to
With her dark eyes a - flash - ing, Cie - li - to
How I long for your touch, my Cie - li - to

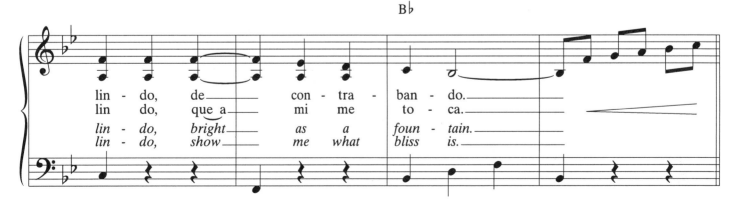

lin - do, de con - tra - ban - do.
lin - do, que a mi me to - ca.
lin - do, bright as a foun - tain.
lin - do, show me what bliss is.

Cielito lindo

Sing in Spanish

It's fun to sing in Spanish. This is the way the words are pronounced in Mexico.

(Verse 1)
De la Sierra Morena,
Deh lah Syeh-rrah Moh-reh-nah,

Cielito lindo viene_en bajando;
Syeh-lee-toh leen-doh vyeh-neh_ehn bah-hahn-doh;

Un par de_ojitos negros,
Oon pahr deh_oh-hee-tohs neh-grohs,

Cielito lindo, de contrabando.
Syeh-lee-toh leen-doh, deh kohn-trah-bahn-doh.

(REFRAIN)
Ay, ay, ay, ay, canta_y no llores;
Ahy, ahy, ahy, ahy, kahn-tah_ee noh yoh-rehs;

Porque cantando se_alegran,
Pohr-keh kahn-tahn-doh seh_ah-leh-grahn,

Cielito lindo, los corazones.
Syeh-lee-toh leen-doh, lohs koh-rah-sohn-ehs.

(Verse 2)
Ese lunar que tienes,
Eh-seh loo-nahr keh tyeh-nes,

Cielito lindo, junto_a la boca;
Syeh-lee-toh leen-doh, hoon-toh_ah lah boh-kah;

No se lo des a nadie,
Noh seh loh dehs ah nah-dyeh,

Cielito lindo, que_a mi me toca.
Syeh-lee-toh leen-doh, keh_ah mee meh toh-kah.

(REFRAIN)

ATF121

Lavender Blue

English Folk Song

Copyright © 1998 by Carl Fischer, Inc.

The Old Gray Mare

American Folk Song

Skip to My Lou

American Folk Song

Moderately

F

Lost   my   part - ner,   what'll   I   do?

C7   F

Skip   to   my   Lou,   my   dar -   ling.

2. I'll find another one, prettier than you,
   I'll find another one, prettier than you,
   I'll find another one, prettier than you,
   Skip to my Lou, my darling.

3. Little red wagon, painted blue,...

4. Can't get a red bird, a blue bird'll do,...

5. Cow in the meadow, moo, moo, moo,...

6. Flies in the buttermilk, shoo, shoo, shoo....

Skip to My Lou

A Circle Game

You can do a circle game with "Skip to My Lou."

1. Form a circle with your friends and choose one person to skip around the outside as every one sings the song and claps the beat.
2. At the end of the verse the "skipper" chooses someone in the circle to join in the skipping, and the two skip around the circle in the second verse.
3. At the end of the second verse the last "skipper" chooses a third person to skip with them.
4. Each new "skipper" chooses another until the end of the song, or until all children are skipping in a circle.

If there are a great many children, all "skippers" can choose another person so that the number of "skippers" doubles each time through. This makes the game go faster.

Polly, Put the Kettle On

American Folk Song

Oh, Dear! What Can the Matter Be?

Scottish Folk Song

Laredo

English Lyric by David Eddleman

Mexican Folk Song

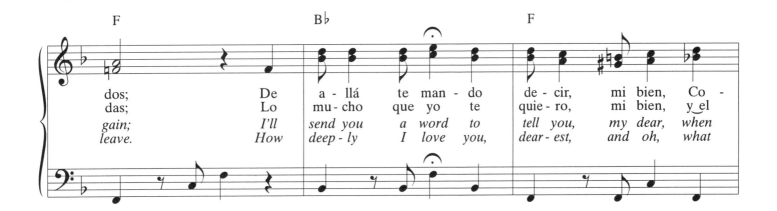

Laredo

Sing in Spanish

Laredo is a town in Texas on the Mexican border. It's right across the Rio Grande River from the Mexican town of Nuevo Laredo. Ask your parents, your teacher, or a librarian to help you find Texas, Laredo, and Nuevo Laredo on a map.

You can sing this song the way Mexican children sing it in Mexico and Texas. The words sound like this.

(VERSE 1)
Ya me voy para_el Laredo, mi bien,
Yah meh bohy pah-rah_ehl Lah-reh-doh, mee byehn,

Te vengo_a decir adiós;
Teh behn-goh_ah deh-seer ah-dyohs;
(Repeat)

De allá te mando decir, mi bien,
Deh ah-yah teh mahn-doh deh-seer, mee byehn,

Como se mancuernan dos.
Koh-moh seh mahn-kwehr-nahn dohs.
(Repeat)

(VERSE 2)
Toma esa llavita de_oro, mi bien,
Toh-mah eh-sah yah-bee-tah deh_oh-roh, mee byehn,

Abre mi pecho y verás;
Ah-breh mee peh-choh ee beh-rahs;
(Repeat)

Lo mucho que yo te quiero, mi bien,
Loh moo-choh keh yoh teh kyeh-roh, mee byehn,

Y_el mal pago que me das.
Ee_ehl mahl pah-goh keh meh dahs.
(Repeat)

My Mama's Calling Me

African American Ring Game

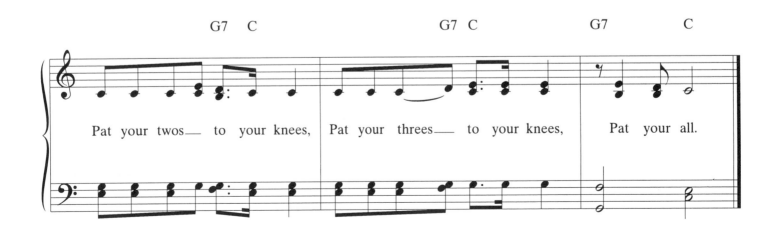

My Mama's Calling Me

A Musical Game

Stand in a circle with some friends. Choose one person to stand in the middle of the circle and be "It." With everyone clapping on the beat, "It" sings *My mama's calling me,* and the others reply *You can't get out o' here.* "It" sings *What shall I do?* Everyone stops clapping and the others reply *Pat your ones to your knees* (everyone, including "It," patting their knees once on the word *pat).* "It" sings again, *What shall I do?* The others reply, *Pat your twos to your knees* (everyone then patting their knees on the words *pat* and *to)* When they sing *Pat your threes to your knees,* everyone pats their knees on the words *pat, threes,* and *to.* When everyone sings *pat your all,* Those forming the circle pat their knees four times as "It" chooses another to take his or her place. The game resumes until everyone has had a chance to be "It."

Red River Valley

Folk Song from the American West

From this val - ley they say you are go - ing, I will miss your bright eyes and sweet smile. For they say you are tak - ing the sun - shine, that has bright - ened our path - way a - while.

2. For a long time, my dear, I've been waiting,
   For those words that you never would say.
   But at last all my fond hopes have vanished,
   For they say you are going away. *(Refrain)*

3. Won't you think of this valley you're leaving,
   And how lonely and sad it will be.
   And think of the heart that you're breaking,
   And the grief that you are causing me. *(Refrain)*

The Farmer in the Dell

Sprightly

Traditional English

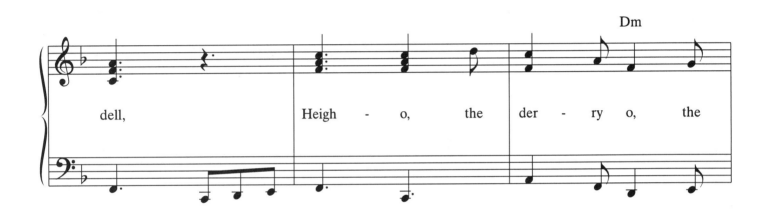

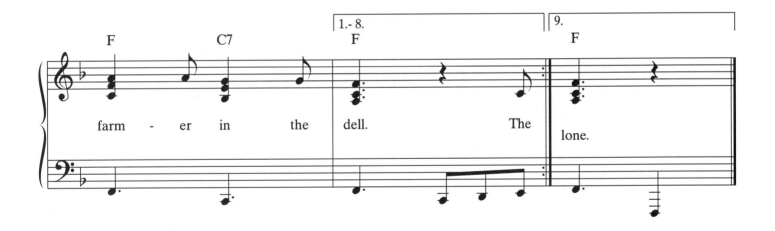

2. The farmer takes a wife,...
3. The wife takes a child,...
4. The child takes a nurse,...
5. The nurse takes a dog,...
6. The dog takes a cat,...
7. The cat takes a rat,...
8. The rat takes the cheese,...
9. The cheese stands alone,...

The Farmer in the Dell

A Game Song

There is a game that goes with this song. Children have played it for many years. Eight children stand in a circle. A ninth person is chosen to be the "farmer," who stands in the center of the circle.

1. In the first verse everyone sings and claps while the "farmer" walks around the inside of the circle.
2. At the end of the verse the "farmer" chooses the person in front of him or her to be the "wife," and they walk around the inside of the circle as everyone sings and claps the second verse.
3. The "wife" then chooses a "child," the "child" chooses a "nurse," and so forth until the "cheese" has been chosen.
4. The other children then form a circle around the "cheese" as they sing *The cheese stands alone*.
5. The "cheese" then becomes the "farmer" and the game continues.

Oats, Peas, Beans and Barley Grow

American Folk Song

Moderately

Oats, peas, beans and bar - ley grow; Oats, peas, beans and bar - ley grow, Can
Here's the farm - er sow - ing seeds, Thus he stands and takes his ease;

you or I or an - y-one know, how oats, peas, beans and bar - ley grow.
Stamp-ing his foot and clasp-ing his hands, he turns a - round and views his lands.

Wait - ing for a part - ner, wait - ing for a part - ner, O - pen the ring and
Tra, la, la, la, la, la, Tra, la, la, la, la, la, Tra, la, la, la, la,

bring one in, While we all gai - ly dance and sing.
la, la, la, Tra, we all la, la, la, la, la, la.

Oats, Peas, Beans, and Barley Grow

Playing a Game

1. Several people stand in a circle holding hands. One person stands inside the circle.
2. As the song is sung, another person walks around the outside of the circle.
3. At the words *Open the ring and bring one in* the circle raises their hands and the "walker" tries to enter the circle under the raised hands.
4. The hands are brought down at the words *While we all gaily dance and sing.* If the "walker" doesn't get into the circle before the hands come down, he or she must continue walking until successfully entering the circle.
5. The people inside the circle choose a new "walker" from among those forming the circle and the game continues until the circle is too small to hold any more "walkers."

When the Saints Go Marching In

African American Spiritual

When the Saints Go Marching In

Marching a March

This song is fun to march to. With your friends, form a line and march. Begin marching on the word *saints,* and start off on your left foot. During the second verse wave your hands in the air as you march. On the third verse, pretend to play a trumpet, a trombone, or a drum as you march.

The second and third verses go like this:

2. Oh, when the stars refuse to shine,...

3. Oh, when I hear that trumpet sound,...

Great Big Stars

African American Folk Song

With spirit

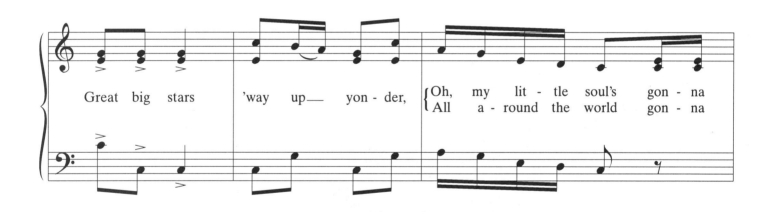

Great Big Stars

Playing a Rhythm

Each time you sing *Great big stars*, you sing the same rhythm

Find a percussion instrument such as a drum or cymbal, or just two sticks that you can tap together. Play the rhythm of *Great big stars* each time you sing it. Then, each time the words *Great big stars* appear, play the rhythm only, without singing, but sing all the other words.

Peace like a River

African American Spiritual

2. I've got joy like a fountain,...
3. I've got love like an ocean,...
4. I've got peace like a river,...

Peace Like a River

PLAYING A "SNAP" RHYTHM

There is a rhythm in this song that may be trickier than you are used to. Some people call it a "snap" rhythm. Each time it appears it's on the word *river*. It looks like this in the music —

riv - er

Can you hear the "snap" in the word *river*? It's a short-long rhythm. Clap the short-long pattern each time you sing *river*. When you clap the second clap (on *-er*) spread your hands apart to show the long note.

La raspa

English Lyric by David Eddleman

Mexican Folk Song

La raspa

A MEXICAN HAT DANCE

In Mexico people sometimes do a dance around a hat. A hat in Spanish is called a *sombrero* (sohm-BREH-roh). Here is a simple version of the dance that you can do with your friends.

Begin by placing a hat in front of you. Stand with your hands on your hips and your feet side by side. In the first section of the song, marked A, you hop on the first, second, and third beats of the song, holding on the fourth beat. On the first beat you hop into this position—your left foot forward and your right foot behind.

On the second beat you hop into a reverse position of your feet, your right foot forward and your left foot behind, and on the third beat you hop back to the first position.
The whole pattern looks like this —

... Hold ...

As the first part of the song goes on you continue the hops, alternating feet each time.

In the second section of the song, marked B, you skip to the left around the hat.

When the first section, the A section of the song comes back, you do the hopping movements again.

To simplify this dance you can do the steps in Section A in halftime, just doing the hopping-to-place steps on the first beat of each measure: *I DANCED and danced and danced. . . la RAS-pa to left and right;. . . So COME and join the dance,. . . Your FEET moving left and right.*

Here is how the Spanish words are pronounced in Mexico.

La raspa yo bailé al derecho y al revés.
Lah rahs-pah yoh bahy-leh ahl deh-reh-choh ee ahl reh-behs.

Si quieres tú bailar, empieza a mover los pies.
See kyeh-rehs too bahy-lahr, ehm-pyeh-sah ah moh-behr lohs pyehs.

Brinca, brinca, brinca también,
Breen-kah, breen-kah, breen-kah tahm-byehn,

mueve, mueve mucho los pies.
mooeh-beh, mooeh-beh moo-choh lohs pyehs.

Que la raspa vas a bailar al derecho y al revés.
Keh lah rahs-pah bahs ah bahy-lahr ahl deh-reh-choh ee ahl reh-behs.

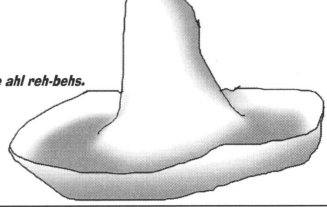

She'll Be Comin' 'Round the Mountain

American Folk Song

Moderately

She'll be com - in' 'round the moun - tain when she comes, ____ She'll be

com - in' 'round the moun - tain when she comes, ____ She'll be com - in' 'round the

moun - tain, She'll be com - in' 'round the moun - tain, She'll be com - in' 'round the

moun - tain when she comes. ____ 2. She'll be comes. ____

2. She'll be drivin' six white horses when she comes,
   She'll be drivin' six white horses when she comes,
   She'll be drivin' six white horses,
   She'll be drivin' six white horses,
   She'll be drivin' six white horses when she comes.

3. Oh, we'll all go to meet her when she comes,
   Oh, we'll all go to meet her when she comes,
   Oh, we'll all go to meet her,
   Oh, we'll all go to meet her,
   Oh, we'll all go to meet her when she comes.

4. We'll be singin' "Hallelujah" when she comes,
   We'll be singin' "Hallelujah" when she comes,
   We'll be singin' "Hallelujah",
   We'll be singin' "Hallelujah",
   We'll be singin' "Hallelujah" when she comes.

She'll Be Comin' 'Round the Mountain

Play the Recorder

Here is a recorder part to play with "She'll Be Comin' 'Round the Mountain" as others sing. You will need the notes G, A, B, and E. E may be a new note for you. It is fingered like this —

Can you see that the part begins with a rest? That kind of rest is called a quarter rest and it means you don't play on that beat. Your first note begins on the syllable *com-*.

Now play this recorder part as others sing.

Goober Peas

Song from the American Civil War

Merrily

Sit-ting by the road-side, on a sum-mer's day, chat-ting with my mess-mates, pass-ing time a-way, Ly-ing in the shad-ow un-der-neath the trees;

Good-ness, how de-li-cious, eat-ing goo-ber peas. Peas, peas, peas, peas, eat-ing goo-ber peas; Good-ness, how de-li-cious, eat-ing goo-ber peas.

Goober Peas

LOOKING IT UP

This funny little song was sung by soldiers during the American Civil War over 130 years ago. Do you know what goober peas are? You probably eat goober peas very often and don't even know it! Ask your parents, your teacher, or a librarian to help you look up the meaning of the word *goober* in a dictionary. You're going to be surprised to find out what it is. When you have learned the meaning of the word *goober* share it with your friends or classmates. Then perhaps your parents will buy you some goobers to eat. They're very healthy. Yum! (Make sure you're not allergic to them. Some people are.)

Work Songs

I've Been Working on the Railroad

(Activity on page 170)

American Folk Song

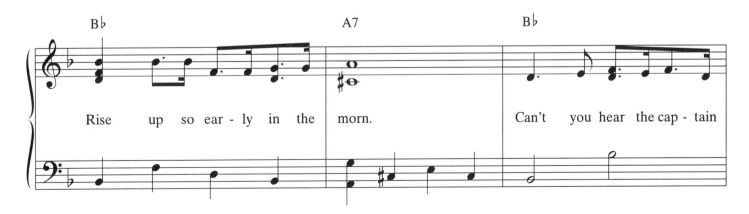

ATF121

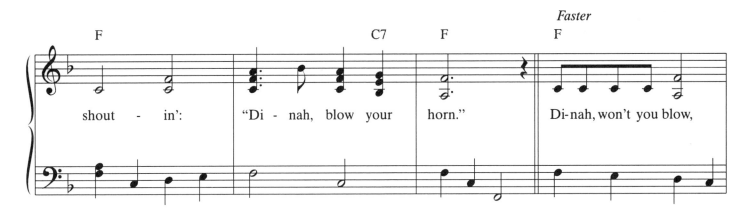

Faster

shout - in': "Di - nah, blow your horn." Di - nah, won't you blow,

Di - nah, won't you blow, Di - nah, won't you blow your horn?_____

Di - nah, won't you blow, Di - nah, won't you blow, Di - nah, won't you blow your

horn?_____ Some - one's in the kitch - en with Di - nah,

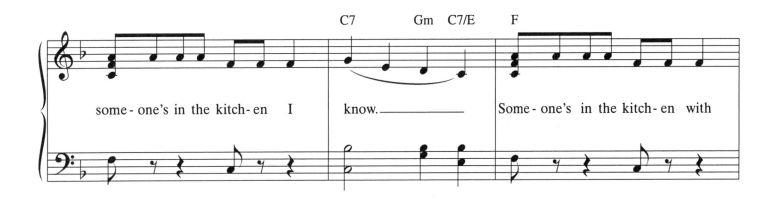

some-one's in the kitch-en I know._____ Some-one's in the kitch-en with

Di - nah, strum-min' on the old ban - jo and sing - in',

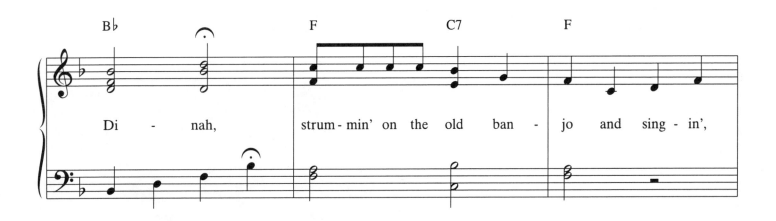

"Fee - fi, fid-dle-ee-i-o, Fee-fi, fid-dle-ee-i - o,_____

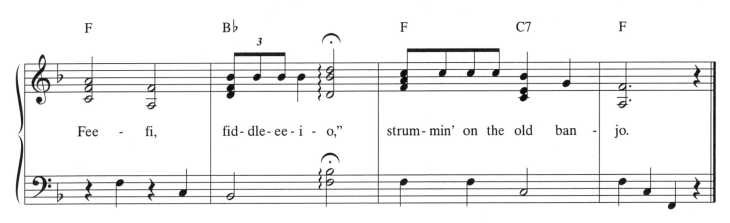

Fee - fi, fid-dle-ee-i-o," strum-min' on the old ban - jo.

I've Been Working on the Railroad

Making a Train Poster

Have you ever ridden on a train? Many years ago, before airplane travel became common, most people who traveled long distances did so on a train. Some trains had dining cars where you could have a meal. Some trains even had small bedrooms so you could sleep while the train clickety-clacked through the night. It must have been a lot of fun!

Do you have old magazines in your house that no one minds your cutting up? Find as many pictures as you can of different kinds of locomotives and trains. Have someone older cut the pictures out and paste them on a single large sheet of heavy paper. Some locomotives run on steam, although there are not many of those left now. Many locomotives run on electricity while others run on diesel fuel, just like some trucks. If you know what kind of locomotive is pulling the train, you can write it underneath its picture. Hang your poster in your room so that others may enjoy it.

Michael, Row the Boat Ashore

African American Work Song

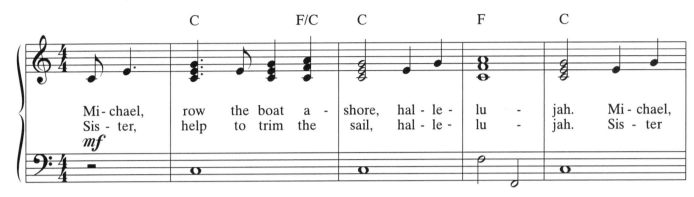

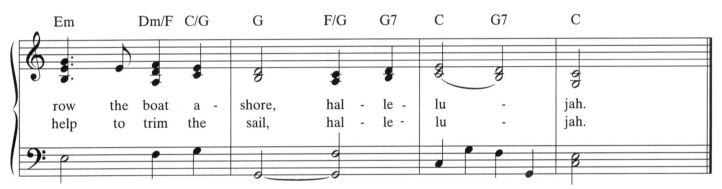

3. Jordan River is chilly and cold, hallelujah.
   Kills the body but not the soul, hallelujah!

4. Jordan River is deep and wide, hallelujah.
   Milk and honey on the other side, hallelujah.

Michael, Row the Boat Ashore

Call and Response

This is a work song, a song that workers sing to help lighten their burden. Probably this song was sung to help workers on boats pull the sails. "Michael, Row the Boat Ashore" is a call-and-response song. Many African American songs use call-and-response. In Africa, it is a very common way to sing a song. In it a leader sings a line and a group responds with a refrain. Sometimes they sing the same line as the leader has sung, but just as often they may sing something different. Choose from among a group of friends someone to act as leader. The leader sings the call (*Michael, row the boat ashore*, or *Sister, help to trim the sails*) and the group responds by singing *Hallelujah*.

ATF121

This Old Hammer

African American Work Song

Copyright © 1998 by Carl Fischer, Inc.

This Old Hammer

Working With a Song

"This Old Hammer" is a work song. Often when workers are doing hard physical labor they will sing songs to make the task easier. Pretend you are working on a railroad track, hammering the huge spikes that hold the tracks in place. Sing the song and pretend to swing the hammer at the end of each phrase — *This old hammer* (swing) *killed John Henry* (swing), and so forth. If you look in the music you will see an *x* above the staff at the end of each phrase. That's where you swing the "hammer."

You can do this with a partner, too. Face your partner and on the swing, swing first to each other's right, then to each other's left. Keep alternating sides throughout the song.

Songs of Freedom

America

Words by
Samuel Francis Smith

Traditional Melody

2. My native country, thee, land of the noble free, thy name I love.
   I love thy rocks and rills, thy woods and templed hills,
   My heart with rapture thrills,
   Like that above.

3. Let music swell the breeze, and ring from all the trees sweet freedom's song.
   Let mortal tongues awake, let all that breathe partake;
   Let rocks their silence break,
   The sound prolong.

4. Our father's God to thee, author of liberty, to thee we sing.
   Long may our land be bright with freedom's holy light,
   Protect us by thy might,
   Great God, our King.

Oh, Freedom

African American Spiritual

3. There'll be singin',...
4. Oh, freedom,...

Oh, Freedom

Looking it Up

Many years ago a man named Dr. Martin Luther King, Jr. led African Americans in an effort to claim the freedoms that were due to them and to all Americans. This song was often sung by Dr. King and the people who worked with him. Go to your library and find out all you can about Martin Luther King, Jr. Your librarian will be happy to help you. Then tell your parents, teachers, friends, or classmates what you have learned. There is a national holiday named for Dr. King. This is a good project to do for Dr. King's holiday. It falls on January 15th each year.

Yankee Doodle

**Words by
Dr. Richard Schuchburgh**

Traditional Melody

Moderately

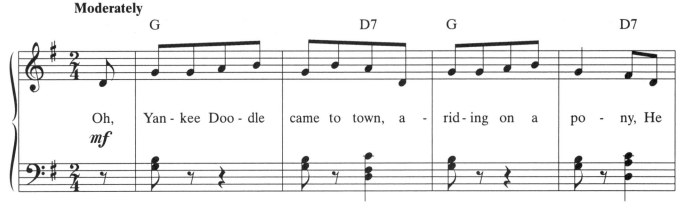

Oh, Yan - kee Doo - dle came to town, a - rid - ing on a po - ny, He

_mf_

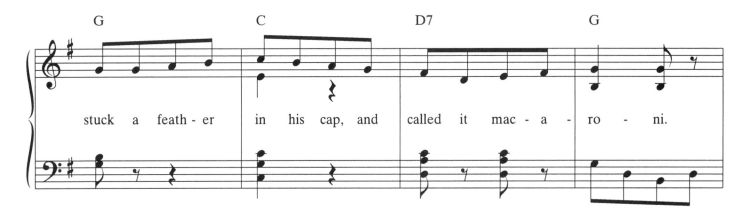

stuck a feath - er in his cap, and called it mac - a - ro - ni.

Yan - kee Doo - dle keep it up, Yan - kee Doo - dle dan - dy;

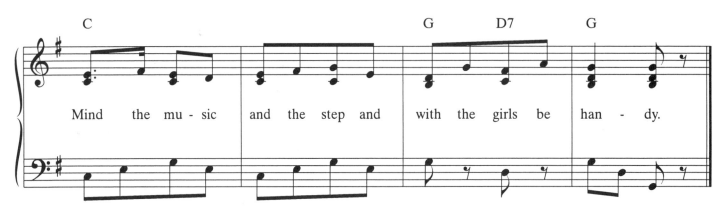

Mind the mu - sic and the step and with the girls be han - dy.

Yankee Doodle

Play the Recorder

You can play a recorder part to go with "Yankee Doodle" using only the notes G, A, and B. Do you remember the fingerings for those notes. Here they are if you need to refresh your memory—

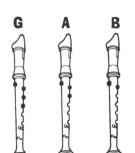

G   A   B

Now try this recorder part as others sing the song. You will see that sometimes you play the melody, but then you will play a harmony part. You may want to practice the rhythm first.

Ev'rybody Ought to Know

African American Folk Song

Ev'rybody Ought to Know

Making an Echo

It's fun to sing echoes in music. With a friend, choose who will start the song. When the first person sings *Ev'rybody ought to know*, the second person echos the words and melody and continues the echoing throughout the song —

Ev'rybody ought to know (E'vrybody ought to know),

Ev'rybody ought to know (Ev'rybody ought to know),

Ev'rybody ought to know (Ev'rybody ought to know),

and then sing together *what freedom is.*

Columbia, the Gem of the Ocean

(Song on page182)

Play the Recorder

This recorder part to go with "Columbia, the Gem of the Ocean" uses only the notes G, A, and B. There is a rhythm in it that you may have seen before in "Peace like a River" on page 158. Sometimes it's called a "snap" rhythm and it looks like this —

You can hear that rhythm when you sing the word *ocean* — short, **l o n g.**

Practice this part, then try playing it with the song as others sing.

Columbia, the Gem of the Ocean

(Activity on page 181)

Words and Music by
D. T. Shaw and T. A. Beckett (1843)

Copyright © 1998 by Carl Fischer, Inc.

2. When war winged its wide desolation, and threatened the land to deform,
The ark then of freedom's foundation, Columbia rode safe thro' the storm.
With the garlands of victory around her, when so proudly she bore her brave crew,
With her flag floating proudly before her, the boast of the red, white, and blue.
The boast of the red, white, and blue; the boast of the red, white, and blue,
With her flag floating proudly before her, the boast of the red, white, and blue.

3. The Star-Spangled Banner bring hither, o'er Columbia's true sons let it wave,
May the wreaths they have worn never wither, nor its stars cease to shine on the brave.
May the service united never sever, but hold to their colors so true,
The Army and Navy forever, three cheers for the red, white, and blue.
Three cheers for the red, white, and blue; three cheers for the red, white, and blue,
The Army and Navy forever, three cheers for the red, white, and blue.

Chapter Contents
and
Subject Index

Chapter Contents

Songs for Any Day

Nursery Rhymes

Weather and Seasons

Our Animal Friends

Silly Songs

Lullabies

Songs From Our Heritage

Work Songs

Songs of Freedom

SUBJECT INDEX

Playing Instruments

Recorder

Percussion

Percussion Instruments

(See Playing Instruments)

Puppets

Recorder

(See Playing Instruments)

Rounds

Sea and River Songs

Sequencing

Story Songs

Traveling

Using the Library

Weather

Working